WHEN THE FLIES SWARM

RICO DIXON

ISBN: 9798815865549

FIRST EDITION

ISBN: 978-0-359-95845-0

DEDICATION

This book is dedicated to my brother, Kibwe Lee, whose motivation and love was always genuine and exactly what was necessary. Your memory will live in my heart forever.

-Acknowledgements-

I would like to acknowledge the people that contributed to this book. I give all praises to Allah for giving me a platform, and the ability to piece these memories together. My grandmother, Doroli B. aka Mimi- for all of your love, strength and faith in me! My aunts, Ava & Monica- for all of your love. To my grandfather- for making me into a man. Thank you! To my brothers, Kenan and Ty- for making me better when I was lost. Thank you, bros. To Ki- for always being my brother, and biggest fan. Save me a spot, brother. To Ms. Lisa Burgess, my editor and mentor- thank you so much for pushing me to get this book done; literally, would not have happened without you. To my godmother, Gwen- for never forgetting your promise to your best friend. To BJ and Marie- for never leaving my side; you two have always been there for me. Love y'all. Napoleon Hill- for "Think and Grow Rich", your legacy shall forever live through me. To Sonja- for dealing with a knucklehead like me. I know it hasn't been easy, but know that you and our kids are my world. Thank you for believing in me. To my children- the reasons I am still here; words cannot express how much you've saved me. I hope that one day you all will understand why I've always been tough on you. I wish you all nothing but the success and abundance that you deserve. Be better than me. To my sister, Shay- I hope that you read this book, and can feel the love I have and always will have for you. I love you. And to my mother, Dorray- I pray that you will one day get to feel what this side of life feels like. I pray that your soul is at peace, and that you will someday find the love you've been desperately seeking. Maybe Allah will leave you some clues, like he did for me. All Praises to the Most High.

-PREFACE-

"It ain't nothing like bruised knees," said Lil' Terrance.

Since we all knew what he meant, we didn't need to say anything. They all stood around me, in a semi-circle, watching me apply a bandage to the gravel-encrusted, gash on my right knee, the effect of falling off a scooter in an alley on Sapp Street. With faces screwed and twisted, they cringed as I pulled off the last piece of dead skin. I cried a little on the inside. I looked at the bandage in my hand. It was already bloody from when I applied it before actually cleaning the cut. I didn't want to use it again, but what other choice did I have? What other choice did any of us have? As I reapplied the bandage, they all began to walk away, going back to their chosen sport. Scooter rides ensued, and skates were put back on. As young as we were, we knew that it wasn't a lot more to 'pain'. You watch it, and get familiar with what it means to see it and to feel it. You recognize it when you see others go through it. You know that this emotion is one that you will encounter time and time again. When you're from a street like Sapp Street, in Baltimore City, you learned to take lessons as they come, and what kind of falls, scrapes, fights, and encounters are waiting for you just around the corner. These corners have been hand-molding the lives of children before and after me. All with bruised knees and bandages that were too cheap to stick.

Chapter 1

It was one of those sleeps. A sleep that should have been deep and heavy. It was a fall, crisp, cool, night, and instead of that deep sleep I'd been yearning for, it was constantly interrupted by noise. Noises from the basement. Laughter that was too loud, screaming that was out of control, and chatter that could be heard throughout the whole house. Somebody must've gotten a good batch, or just didn't care that I had to go to school in the morning, because nobody seemed to care that I needed to be asleep.

By that fall, my mother was barely filling her shifts at the Post Office, and our house became the "Party House". My mother went from selling a few dime bags of grass here and there, to being one of the best local suppliers for coke on our side of North Avenue. She and her boyfriend, Kevin, were making good money; enough to let people come to our house, on school nights, to party and get away from the realities of their own households. Even at that age, I did not approve.

To get to the bathroom in our two- bedroom house, you had to come through my room and they always had to pee. Some would try to be quiet as they walked through and some would continue their conversations as if I weren't in there trying to sleep. Whether they were quiet or not, those hardwood floors ALWAYS woke me up. And once I was up, I was up. I usually used the noise as an excuse to sneak down the thirty-nine steps it took to get to the basement, just to get a glimpse of the parties. I was just a kid wanting to see all the fun. A glimpse of the cocaine, the laughter, the music, and the chaos.

The cigarette smoke always got stronger as you got closer to the people. My mother was always the loudest, with her red lipstick, bright smile, and her signature 'mushroom' hairstyle. She was the life of the party. I usually was able to stand there for five minutes before anybody even noticed me. I was fascinated at how carefree and happy they all looked. It was like they didn't have a care in the world and I guess with their full ashtrays, drinks, and white noses, maybe they didn't. At least not at that time. I wasn't familiar with any of these people and each night seemed to bring different faces. I would wonder where their kids were and why they never bought them over to play with me. Or if I was just lucky enough to live in the Party House.

By the time my mother spotted me one night, I was completely focused on the two men sniffing white lines off of the table.

"What are you doing down here, boy?" she asked. The people began scrambling to hide their illegal's, until they saw that it was just the boy from upstairs. When they realized it was just "D's" son, they sighed relief and continued to put the white powder up their noses with the rolled dollar bill. It was no longer important to hide their secrets.

She always made me say goodnight to everybody before taking the hike back up to the top floor. As we crept into the darkness, she would say quietly, "Take this money, and buy yourself some candy tomorrow." She would slide me a one-dollar bill in the darkness, and kiss me on the forehead. I remember how her clothes smelled as she walked away, like Johvan Musk, and cigarettes, only to leave me to fall asleep before the sun came up, and just after the party ended. There were always two things that I felt before I opened my eyes; that dollar bill and complete confusion. I didn't understand how things had gone from me and Mommy being so close and happy, to what it had now become. I didn't understand how it had gone from me and Mommy, to me, Mommy, and a bunch of strangers. I didn't understand why they were always at *my* house. Confusion.

Walks to school were always cool to me. I was able to get my main man Tony to walk with me. Tony was a year older than I was, and he had a stutter. He was always good to me. He always helped me if he saw that I was struggling, or giving me high fives throughout the day at school, or telling me that things would be ok. Kids with drug addicted parents seemed to be very cold and hard, but not Tony. He always looked out for me even through his own adversity. Tony was always a smiling face, and smiling faces came very seldom. Our mothers were friends and although Mommy's use hadn't gotten out of control, Tony's mom's heroin addiction was all over the place and they were often without electricity or food. Mommy tried to help with food when she could but sometimes things were just bad.

Before school, Tony and I would always stop at the corner store for junk food; you know, penny candy, a huggee juice, and some party mix. We would rush the candy bags into our backpacks as we ran to the last door on the school yard leading into the building. Cecil Elementary was my school and they stressed that our uniforms, white polo shirts and navy khaki pants, had to be clean at all times. I LOVED school. I loved learning, I loved knowing the answers to everything, and knowing how to read faster than most of the students. I hated the fact that most of my classmates were never in school on a daily basis though. By this time, drugs were very prevalent in my neighborhood, and you could tell that their effects trickled down to the kids as well. When a kid missed school, you knew that most likely, they weren't at the doctor or the dentist. Most likely, a mom or dad was passed out or something worse and they would not return for a few days. Sometimes when Tony was out of school, I worried if he and his little brother were alright and I worried for his mom.

I had a classmate named Vera, a little mixed girl with a white mother and a black father. Vera's homelife was rare but only in the sense that she still had both of her parents in the same house. Both of her parents were addicts. A lot of the other kids teased her saying that her skin was yellow because she peed on herself and she smelled like urine. They called her "Piss Pot." It was rumored that her mother was a prostitute and she got teased for that. Her clothes were dingy and her hair was unkept, often in a finger combed ponytail that looked as if she did it herself. And to make things worse, Vera had a speech impediment and spoke as if she may have been deaf. Although Vera was very smart, she had no friends and never took her eyes off the floor. She held her head down and cried. I felt bad for her. I could never tease another person. Not ever. Vera's family must have moved because she was transferred out in the fall. Where I would see her again would touch my heart forever.

Chapter 2

Friday nights were the BEST!! That meant it was time for me to go to my godmother's house. She was known as Gwen, but I called her "Godmommy". Going to her house meant McDonald's and the newest happy meal toy, playing with my godsisters, and finding new things to get into. It meant staying up late, ghost stories and above all, it meant Tisha.

Tisha was our baby sitter. She was about sixteen, light skinned, brown hair, big, brown eyes, slender frame, and a beautiful bright smile. I thought she was beautiful. She always knew just what to say. "Come here, Boyfriend," she would scream when she saw me. "Did you miss me," she would always ask when I jumped in her arms. I always missed her. She made me blush with her words and, as a kid, it felt real. She would let me sit on her lap when we watched movies and she would pick me up and carry me in her arms. I knew that she loved me.

I had no idea where my mother would disappear to on those nights and I really didn't care. I was with my sisters and Tisha. They loved having me around and I loved being around them. My godmother treated me like a king, because I was the only boy. The boy that I think she secretly always wanted but never had. We always had a GREAT time on those weekends. We'd get up early on Saturday mornings, eat McDonald's signature Big Breakfasts' meals, talk to each other about make-believe friends, learning new games. It was perfect back then.

As much as I loved being at Godmommy's house, sometimes I was confused as to why I was there. My mom worked during the week and was off on weekends so I didn't understand why she dropped me off over there. Weekends used to be for us. Weekends used to be our time together, hanging out, watching movies, and just being together. But now it seemed that I was at Godmommy's every weekend, as if Mommy didn't want me around. Almost as if she had to have me during the week for school, but weekends were for her and her only.

The vibe in the house from my godmother would start to get strange if I was still there Sunday evening. She never said anything but I could feel the change. It's not like she didn't want me there but she had to get her children ready for school the next day and now, instead of dinner for two children, she had an extra mouth. Sometimes Mommy didn't come for me until sunrise on Monday mornings, which caused rightful irritation because I shouldn't have been there.

Mommy would come get me, and look so tired, like she had been working extra shifts at the Post Office. I often tricked myself into believing that's where she'd been.

***

My father was a slim man, very dark, slick hair, like that of a Mexican, and reddish colored skin, an American Indian. He spoke very softly, with a slow, slurred, dragging voice. The voice of a heroin addict. My mother left him when I was just four months old. She was working for The Naval Academy at the time and came home after a twelve-hour shift to hear me crying upstairs. As she climbed the flights of stairs to get me, she knew that something was terribly wrong. My cry was too hard for just a wet diaper or feeding time. She arrived to find me stretched out on the bed, screamimg, next to an overdosed father. I was told that the needle was still in his arm when she found us. She smacked him hard a few times to get him to come to and eventually he did. My mother was about three months pregnant at the time with my little sister, who they would name after my mother, Dorray, but due to complications from my father's heroin use, the pregnancy was terminated.

Charles would come around every now and again, to make fake promises. Promises that left me sitting on my steps for HOURS, waiting for him to come and get me. I would often try to count the stars before he came. The stars would always make me tired enough to play sleep when my mother would come and check on me. She would put me on her shoulder, and carry me inside.

She was a good mother to me. She was always attentive and showed me lots of love and affection. She worked good jobs and had stability with The Naval Academy and the Post Office. She was responsible and always had extra money. She worked hard during the week and the weekends belonged to us. She would take me to get crabs and we'd meet up with some of her friends and their kids downtown. We would go to the store and just hang out. She always made sure I was dressed in the latest clothes and always had a nice haircut. Mommy was big on education and always told me how smart I was. She read to me every night before bed and always encouraged me to read for myself. Because of this, I won an award for being the youngest reader in the school. I was in kindergarten and was reading on a third-grade level. She was always so proud of me. I was her world and she was mine. Mommy was beautiful. Men loved her and women wanted to be her. She had many friends and was always willing to help anyone when she could. I remember one day, we were walking to the store and a friend of hers stopped, whispered something in Mommy's ear, and Mommy went into her purse and handed the lady a few dollars. Everybody loved her.

But, now, I felt her fading. Fading into the darkness of our neighborhood. You know the signs; I would wake up in the middle of the night, and she would be gone, leaving me asleep, people coming by the house that I'd never seen before.

Then I noticed something was different about her. She would come and get me from school early and when we got home, she would just sleep. She would say she was just tired. I thought maybe she was sick but her appetite was healthy. Her passionate nature was returning. She was becoming more affectionate towards me and I could see her natural glow beginning to come back. Maybe she was beginning to slow down and things would go back to how they once were. I even walked in on a few conversations she and Kevin would have about moving and about them trying to get away from their problems in Baltimore. They wanted to get away from all the drugs and dealers and increasing crime. They wanted a fresh start.

I was wrong. Mommy hadn't slowed down her drug use. Mommy wasn't coming back to herself. Mommy wasn't hugging me more out of love and attention. Mommy wasn't eating because she was getting healthy. Mommy wasn't clinging to Kevin because she was so in love. Mommy was a statistic about to bring another statistic into the world.

Mommy was pregnant.

I was angry.

I was mad.

I was nervous.

I was confused.

This was stupid! How could she even want to bring a baby into this chaos?! We were barely surviving and she wants a baby?! She wasn't the same mother that she was when I was born. She was stable then. I barely recognized this woman as my mother. The thought of a new baby made me nervous. Nervous because I was already practically raising myself and I knew that most of the responsibility would fall on me. Mommy would party and I would take care of the baby. I just didn't understand.

The mornings seemed to last later that spring. I woke up to breakfast again. I guess Mommy was feeling maternal. The parties continued, but they just didn't seem as reckless anymore. There weren't as many people showing up, they didn't stay as late, and they weren't as loud. I noticed that Mommy wasn't partying as hard as before. Maybe there was hope.

I liked walking to school with just a light jacket on and being able to feel the sun on my face. Feeling the warm sun on my skin made moments like this very refreshing. It was a reminder that you were alive and that there was light after darkness. Even if it was only temporary.

I spent a lot of time with my maternal grandmother, Mimi, around those times, and she would take me to the library. We would read for hours in the library, where it was quiet, and then go back to her house and watch movies that we'd rented. Some of the movies were comical and some were educational, but it didn't matter to me, I just loved spending that time with her.

My grandmother's goal was to always keep me exposed to different heritages, different cultures, and different ways of life. She would teach me morals, and values, traditions, and love. She was the closest thing to perfection that I ever knew. We would often go to Towson Library, an affluent community outside of the city limits, where she would leave me to roam through the countless aisles of children's books. Because of these visits, I would learn to read very well before age six. We would rent movies, well, they were actually free movies that you could check out like books with your library card, and go back to her house to relax and have movie night. We would make cookies together, and act silly. It was a welcomed reprieve from my everyday life with my mother.

Mimi treated me like I was important.

My grandmother was a person that could find the beauty in ANY living soul. She believed that her bad neighborhood would someday be quiet again. She hated seeing her people strung out on drugs, and weak. She marched and protested with the NAACP back in the 1960's. She was old school. She always commanded respect and appropriate behavior; yet, she was cool at the same time by allowing you to express yourself and even letting you choose the radio station in the car. She taught me about slavery, and South Africa, and how to properly answer questions. She taught me how to read fast, and how to think even faster.

She treated me like I was important.

After the weekends with my grandmother, I went back home; back to the Party House. At the end of the school year and before the heat of the summer, I noticed my mother and Kevin arguing a lot more. His drug use became more prevalent, and his efforts to hide it was getting sloppy. Real sloppy. He was beginning to get careless and thoughtless by leaving all the evidence of his habit just laying around the house. He didn't care if I saw it

or even came across it.

Chapter 3

I slept hard that night, the night that I grew up. I slept hard enough to dream, with a box fan blowing from the corner of my room. I heard voices that sounded blurry, voices that sounded angry, and all too familiar. I opened my eyes to a dull darkness and the summer moon bouncing off of the wall. The arguing was coming from my mother's room. There was a smell in the air. A smell that was constantly present. A thick marijuana haze.

"Bitch, what's his name?!" Kevin shouted.

I could tell by the tone of his voice that he was very angry, and I immediately was overcome with fear. I slowly turned the doorknob to my mother's room and saw him leaning atop of her on the edge of the bed. She was pregnant, crying, and had a sweaty forehead. Crack pieces sat on the nightstand, the lampshade off of the lamp tossed on the floor. And there was a noticeable haze of white smoke in the air. The smoke was so thick that I gagged when I came in. She was wearing her fuzzy pink robe. He was leaning over and screaming at her about the guy that I noticed coming by the house to drop off drugs. Kevin thought that there was more to their relationship than just the buying and selling of crack.

"Do you be sucking that nigga dick!?" He screamed.

"What, Kevin? Calm down," she shrieked.

"Well, Bitch, since you like sucking that nigga dick, then come on, suck mine!" He shouted.

He pulled his pants down, proceeding to pull his penis out of his pants, grabbing the back of her head in a demanding gesture to do as he asked.

"Suck it!" He screamed.

"My son is standing right there, Kevin!" She said.

"I don't give a fuck! Suck my dick!" He said, grabbing her hair, forcing her mouth onto his penis.

Not thinking, I ran to my room and grabbed the first thing that I felt in the darkness. It was a baseball bat that one of her friends had given to me. I ran back into the room with the bat above my head and swung it as hard as I could, trying to kill him with all my might. I was crying at this point, shouting, "Get off of my motha!" He grabbed the bat from me and pushed me on the ground. The splinters from the jagged wood floor pierced my right side, thigh, and leg.

My mother was able to run away to the steps, where she fell next to the landing. He pushed his way to her. I grabbed him pushing, and scratching, punching with all of my strength, but he made his way to her. Just as she reached for the rail to the steps, I slid in front of him, trying to stop him or slow him down. This made him slap me so hard that I fell down all twenty- six steps that led upstairs. The same steps that taught me how to count.

The blow left my eyes blurry, and my face numb. I watched that pink robe run over me, and out of our front door, with him chasing behind her, screaming obscenities and calling her names. I lay on that floor wondering if I was still alive and if this was still a part of the dream that I was having just a few minutes ago. I wondered what would happen if he killed her. I felt weak. I could hear my mother screaming, running up and down our tiny street, "Somebody call the police!"

He beat my mother on the side of our house. By the time I was able to get to the front door, she was struggling to stand. Five and a half months pregnant, with a bloody face, bruised skin, and a confused son crying alone on the moonlit street. No neighbors came to help. No superheroes came from the shadows. No police. No one. Just us. We climbed the steps together, until we finally felt the edges of the crush velvet couch in our living room, wondering what was to come next. Neither one of us knew where Kevin went after he beat her, we just knew that he wasn't there. And for the remainder of that night, we were safe.

I watched the sunrise that morning as my mother slept on the couch. But this was the first time, at just six years old, I watched the sun rise, through the eyes of a man.

-Interlude-

Her habit started like everyone else's, out of curiosity. She'd smoked some grass in college and even tried PCP but didn't like it. Her godfather was a dealer. She was with him one day and saw him making his supply. This was during the time when people started to cook cocaine and turned it into rocks for smoking. She asked him what it was and he told her that it was rock cocaine and asked her if she wanted to try it. She did and instantly liked it. The next time she saw him, he gave her more and she liked it even more. They say you can get hooked on crack after the first time. It took her after the second time.

Not seeing her godfather anymore, she went to the streets to find it.

The change was quick after she started. Almost overnight. She missed work and got fired. She stopped walking me to school, she stopped making breakfast. She got sluggish and lazy and all she wanted to do was sleep. I would come home from school and the cable would be off. I never thought the cable would be off. Or the phone.

Before her addiction, I was a typical, happy, vibrant kid. I liked to play and laugh and have a good time. I didn't have a care. I even felt lucky because I wasn't going through what other kids were going through with their families. My mom wasn't like theirs. And then, she was. The change was quick within me. Almost overnight. I became irritable and short fused. Snappy. I was angry. I was hurt. I was mad. I started ignoring her or just walking away when she talked. I rolled my eyes or sucked my teeth in response. She didn't deserve respect from me anymore.

She was a disappointment. I was disappointed.

Chapter 4

She was born on a cold, rainy night, October 26th 1990. I stood there looking through a small window of the delivery room, when she came into this world. Her father and I stood speechless. Shelae Shenae Mosley had arrived. She had a head like an egg, bright eyes, and the most innocent smile I had ever seen in my entire life.

I got to see her up close as my mom and Kevin were talking to the doctors. I just stood looking at her. She was finally here. Something needed to be discussed and Kevin asked me to leave the room for a few minutes. He asked me to leave the room like I didn't already know what was going on. As I left, I heard the doctors whisper something to my mother about her addiction during the pregnancy. It was humiliating. I walked back to the window, where I could see my little sister moving around in her clear bassinet, wondering what had just happened and why did

THESE have to be her parents. By the time it was alright for me to come back into the room, I felt completely numb.

Those days went by in a blur, as family members came and went to and from the hospital. Financially, we were still just trying to make it. Mentally and emotionally, I didn't see how we were going to make it. With a new baby at home, I thought that for sure things would calm down at the Party House. Once again, I was wrong.

Most nights, I slept in my mother's bed with Shay. She didn't have a crib and I was afraid of leaving her alone. My mother always insisted that I needed to go into my own room. But I hated the smoke coming all the way upstairs on Shay so, I thought that I was "protecting" her by breathing in all the smoke for her first. My mother would be downstairs with her friends, snorting lines, and smoking crack. She would walk up the stairs and her shirt, forehead, and collar were drenched in sweat. Her lips would be mangled. She could barely talk, like there was somebody holding her tongue, and there were cotton balls in her cheeks. Her eyes moved fast and she could not stay still. She was pacing the floor and fidgeting with everything. She just couldn't be still. What hurt the most was that she could never look at me.

Like I wasn't important.

She would always look at the floor, like she was searching for something. She would always think I was asleep, and I would peer at her through my sheets. She disgusted me. Embarrassed me. Some nights, she would make sure Shelae was asleep, and slide me a dollar bill, like the old days. But I didn't want anything that came from her. The gesture just wasn't the same anymore. It was like she was a shell. A shell of somebody with so much life.

She would come up those steps, smelling like the basement; cigarettes, sweat and feet, and smoke, and nail polish remover; like burning cotton balls and candle wax.

She seemed so lost, so absent- minded, so caught up in the life downstairs that she was disconnected from the real world upstairs. It would be so late and she would come and ask me questions about my homework, as if she cared. She used that as more of a distraction than concern. I knew that she no longer cared about herself, and even less about us.

I learned how to cry silently that winter. I learned how to talk to myself, and to imagine the things that I read in the books with my grandmother. Shelae fell off of the bed a lot of times that winter. Those falls left a lot of bruises on her head; bruises that I would have to lie about to my grandmother and godmother on the weekends. After so many bruises and lies, Mimi bought Shay a crib.

The sky seemed extra dark that winter. I don't remember Christmas. I don't remember New Years. All I remember is the Party House. And moving into my grandmother's house. My mother sold my Atari, she sold my leather jacket, she sold Shelae's crib. She sold our televisions. With all that was sold, no rent was paid. We lost our home.

She went from being the supplier, to the crack fiend. We lost everything. I left Cecil Elementary School. My friends. Sapp Street. My neighbors. The velvet couch. My memories. As many times as I watched my mother get beat in that house, heard the sexual expletives of strange men in that house after Kevin left, heard lighters flick to crack pipes in that house, as ugly as it was, it was home.

I left some of myself there.

Chapter 5

That spring was a typical one, in the sense of weather. The mornings were cool, afternoons were warm, and the sunsets lasted longer. Shelae and I moved into my grandmother's house. Mommy never moved in with us and we didn't know where she was staying. Mimi gave me the little room, and let Shelae have the biggest room. Shelae had a new crib, and I now attended Matthew A. Henson Elementary, a school in the heart of West Baltimore. My grandmother found a day care that would keep Shelae during the day and I would go there after school until Mimi would come get us. Most mornings, Mimi would drop me off at school and then go to work. I didn't wear white shirts and navy pants anymore because the new uniform was gold shirts, and navy pants. This idea made Mimi thankful, because she only had to buy different shirts. My shoes weren't new anymore. My smile wasn't real anymore.

Most days in school, I didn't even speak to any of the other kids. I did not fit in at my new school. These kids were ruthless. They cursed, they fought and they didn't seem to care about learning. I would walk to the day-care after school by myself.

I witnessed a lot on those walks home. I saw my first "Tester Lines", which are lines where heroin addicts would line up for a free sample of new packages on the street. I saw a child get hit by a car one evening. It was so crazy to me. The boy was one of the kids that went to my school. He was crossing the street with two other kids in his class, when a green Thunderbird struck him, and kept going. I didn't understand how someone could just hit him and keep going. What disturbed me more was that when they hit him, he got stuck and they dragged his body for about two blocks before stopping. And when they stopped, it was only to unhook his body. Not to see if he was okay or to call for help, just to unhook him. And then, they just left him there. I ran over only to see him bleed out on the ground. His eyes rolled in his head, arms stretched above his head. He was an older kid. I did not know for sure if he survived the hit and run, but I don't see how anyone could.

I walked to the day-care, where Ms. Cathy would curse at us, telling us to get in the damn yard or shut the hell up. She fed us microwaved ravioli's every afternoon. She would throw shoes at us, to get our attention, and she would always be on the phone when I got to the house.

She treated me like I wasn't important.

She would yell at my sister for being a baby, like telling her to shut up when she was crying. She would tell us that she couldn't stand us, and that she had better things to do. She would always say that five o'clock needed to hurry up so she could be rid of us. She always made me feel like Shay and I were a burden. She must have forgotten that she was being paid to watch us. Ms. Cathy lived off of North and Fulton, deep in Baltimore City and just two blocks away from where my father lived. I hated it there. She would make us sit on the floor until our parents came and we would be forced to watch "The Never-Ending Story"; a movie that I was too young to understand, and it made my head hurt. One Thursday afternoon, I walked into the makeshift day-care, only to hear a familiar voice.

A voice that was unforgiving,

A voice that was cold.

A voice that was frigid.

A voice that belonged to my mother.

I walked in to see her sitting down, with a blank look on her face as she talked to Ms. Cathy. I was immediately happy to see her and I ran to her, but she didn't seem as happy to see me. She was holding a sleeping Shelae in her lap. She told Ms. Cathy that she needed to talk to me alone and thanked her for looking after us. She told me that she had a surprise for me, and that we needed to go outside.

The air was chilly, as the sun set over the city. She was noticeably skinnier as we walked out of the wooden back gate of the day-care.

"I got some candy for you, but no money," she said.

I nodded my head like I understood.

"Devin, there are a lot of things that happen to us, that you will understand when you are older. I just need you to trust me," she said.

We continued to walk towards North Avenue, and I opened my candy bag with a sick feeling in my stomach. Something major was happening, like I knew that she was here to tell me bad news. As she began to talk, I noticed that she had several bags thrown over her shoulder. Those bags were Shelae's.

We walked up to North Avenue, where everybody was buzzing back and forth, and the dirt bikes passed us making loud noises. I couldn't hear anything that she was saying to me and she never looked at me. Finally, once we got to the corner, she grabbed my hand, and kneeled down to my eye level. She had Shelae on her shoulder, with a blanket over her head.

"I got to go baby. And your grandmother is going to bring you to me in a little while."

I swallowed hard, and squeezed her hand even harder. "But where-" I started.

"Baby, you will understand when you get there. And you're gonna be fine. I just gotta do this for ME. For us," she interrupted.

She leaned close to me, held me for a few seconds, and kissed me on my cheek before letting me go. I remember smelling her perfume and cigarette smoke on her collar. She was leaving me, again, with no regret, no sorrow, and a straight face. She held my hand as she flagged down the number five bus coming towards us. She let my hand go and said she would call me, right before the bus doors opened. She boarded the crowded bus with Shelae, and her clothes, and her bottles, and her diapers.

She was leaving me like I didn't matter.

Like I wasn't important.

The exhaust fumes of that bus were strong as they blew in my face on that cool evening. I wished that the bus would stop as I stared at the next stop just one block away. But it never did. I watched the bus go farther away from me until I couldn't see it anymore. I started walking back towards Ms. Cathy's house with tears in my eyes, throwing the gum away that she had just given me. My head ached and my throat had a lump, but I knew that I couldn't let those tears fall. I didn't know what to do. Or what to feel. Or where to go. Or where I belonged.

This was the first time that I felt alone, scared, and worthless, all at the same time. I sat on Ms. Cathy's stoop in a lethargic state, eating penny candy, staring into the nothing on Fulton Avenue. I knew that this time, she was gone and there was nothing that I could do about it. And that the one thing that gave me a reason to stay strong was gone too. Shelae.

I was a seven-year-old boy with a cold heart and a spirit that was too broken to appreciate a lousy sunset in a busy city.

That night, my soup spoon echoed in the dining room of my grandmothers' house. I tried hard not to look at my sister's play pen out of the corner of my eye. I kept imagining that she was just asleep, and that the entire day was a dream. My grandmother was very quiet and that was odd for her because she loved to talk and often asked about the activities of my day. She met me at Ms. Cathy's, only to find that Ms. Cathy LET my mother take my sister without her permission. I was sure that tonight would be the last time I'd ever see Ms. Cathy. I was right.

That night my grandmother let me wash myself up, and let me sleep in her bed with her. I felt incomplete.

Shelae should have been there, with us, instead of somewhere with Mommy. I know I was being selfish but that's what I felt. Mimi was a bit overwhelmed at times with us and Ms. Cathy just didn't care, but she was still better off with us. I was worried about where my sister was, and if my mother knew how to feed her; how to hold her; how to be patient with her. I wondered if she knew not to smoke around her or not to make loud noises around her. Thoughts like those made me cry myself to sleep. I learned how to cry silently into a pillow. And to make myself believe in dreams.

I dreamed that Shay was just fine, and so was my mother, and that maybe she met some millionaire who had a limousine that picked them up from somewhere. And that maybe, someday that millionaire would send for me too. I held on to the sweet kisses Shay would leave on my cheek in the mornings; how our eyes looked the same when we would laugh together; how she was my everything in a small person. She was the only thing that was the same for me. The day she left, was the day that changed my life. It was then that I experienced a deeper level of emptiness.

Chapter 6

Two months passed since the day they left. I had grown an inch or two and my mother "kind of" kept her word. She said, just before she left, that she would call me and that she would keep in touch. She called my grandmother's home after being missing for nearly 30 days. Well, it turns out, somebody had seen Mommy during her binges and took her to my godmother, Gwen. My godmother took her to DSS (Department of Social Services), and Mommy told DSS that she wanted to go anywhere there were Section 8 vacancies. There were vacancies in South Carolina and that's where she went. She said that she found sobriety in South Carolina. There was a family at a church there, that was willing to let her live with them, while she got on her feet. And she was ready for me to join them after the school year had come to a close.

She and my grandmother would cry on the phone together until the wee hours of the night. My mother would tell her of the sunsets that she was able to witness in Myrtle Beach, and the powerful messages at her nightly Narcotics Anonymous meetings. She was clean and sober. She told my grandmother how much she did not miss the big city of Baltimore, and how overwhelmingly FREE she felt there in South Carolina. She eventually gave my grandmother the green light to bring me to her. She said that she had a place for us, and a new job, and a church home. She was ready to become someone.

My aunts helped me pack oversized duffel bags and told me stories of how beautiful the weather was gonna be in the south. We picked a sweet watermelon from Stop, Shop & Save before getting on the highway. We sang, laughed, and joked for the duration of the ride. I often found myself lost in conversation with myself as I stared out onto the highways of the south. The air was different.

The license plates were different. And so was the feeling. My grandmother told me that I would have a longer summer than the kids I left behind. And that this was MY start to something great.

She made me feel like I was important.

I saw "South of The Border" billboards. These are famous billboards that you only see when driving to the south. South of the Border is actually a rest area that has restaurants, mini golf, arcade, and all types of fun things to do while you were resting from a long drive.

I felt an anxious pit in the bottom of my stomach from the excitement. It seemed as if we couldn't get there fast enough. I wore a neon green fanny pack, with three pieces of gum that was in the candy bag Mommy gave me before she left, that I'd been saving for two and a half months, a pack of tissues, and a keychain that I won from being in the Book Club at school. I saved the gum, so that Shay and I could chew a piece together, even though she barely had teeth; a pack of tissues, in case my mother would cry when she saw us, and a keychain to show her what I'd accomplished since she'd been away. When it came time to get out of the Chevy Nova though, all of my plans that I had, left my mind as easily as they had wandered in. As I walked around trying to calm my nervousness, I stared at a huge statue of a mexican man with a black sombrero. My grandmother snapped pictures as I wandered around, but then, and just then, I heard something that would change my life again.

"Is that my baby right there?"

I knew that voice. Though it'd been forever since I heard it, I knew that voice. It was the voice of my sober mother. The one that recognized me from far away. The one that knew what my voice sounded like. The one that missed me as much as I missed her.

The one that treated me like I was important.

It was her, with a white shirt, and jogging pants, glasses on her eyes, and that mushroom hairstyle. A smile that I could pick out of any room. A smile that I knew from anywhere. She stood in the sand with her arms wide open and just enough room for ME to finally fit inside. I slowly ran to her, trying my hardest to hold in my tears. She hugged me tight, like she didn't want to ever let me escape her grasp again.

Like I was important.

Time faded away in those moments. Like God stopped every wristwatch in the world for just a few moments. When I finally released my head that I buried into her shoulder, I opened my eyes to see Shay. My grandmother held her, and I ran straight to her. She was OK. I squeezed her hard, and kissed her cheeks. She laughed, as I looked over her hands to still count ten fingers. I looked up to see two eyes, and a clean face. I was happy to see that she was perfectly fine. I cried so much that afternoon, that "South of The Border" on the billboard was a blur, as were the conversations and pictures. All I knew is that I was where I belonged and that I had a lot to be grateful for. It was finally my turn to see what it felt like to be loved by my mother with a full heart, sober mind and true eyes. All I could do was thank God. After a lot of tears and goodbyes, it was time to begin the next chapter of our lives together, just the three of us. Afraid, eager, excited and sad, I said goodbye to Aunt Ava, Aunt Monica and to Mimi, my grandmother, who looked so happy to see us all reunited. I was happy to be with Mommy but sad to leave Mimi at the same time.

One of my mother's friends from the church loaded all of my bags into the back of his white Ford Ranger. He was a nice man, with a clean-shaven face. He was brown skinned, with a slim build and proper speech. He kind of reminded me of a southern football coach dressed a polo style shirt, khaki slacks, and a cap. He told me about the journey that Shay and my mother had endured to get to his church. He told me that Mommy had been having second thoughts about moving to South Carolina and kept wanting to get off the bus during the trip. Apparently when she finally made it to town, she was lost and the DSS office had closed for the day. After such a hard day and feeling defeated, she was able to get food and find shelter at the church that night. Mommy's journey started out tough but she got settled and now she was here. He also told me how thankful he was to have me here with them. He said that South Carolina was a beautiful place to start over again and that I would fit in just fine. We drove past mountains, palm trees and many wooded areas to get to our destination. I told my mother how much I missed her and Shay, and how good I was doing in school back in Baltimore. It was perfect. She said that we would be staying at her friend's house that she met in church, who was also a recovering drug addict, with three sons of her own.

We arrived at a development with all townhomes, and trees, with at least four playgrounds that I could count when we entered the community. The trees were all pine trees, and the air smelled fresh, nothing like back at home. Everyone's accents were thick and country and I was excited to see my new room, and my new home.

My excitement was short lived.

Chapter 7

Mommy said that we would have our own place, our own space, with good schools, and friendly neighbors. What she didn't mention was that she, Shay and I would be sharing a small bedroom together. She also DIDN'T tell us that this friend we would be living with, Ms. Betty, had relapsed and started drinking again. She never told us how prejudiced the south was, and about all the confederate flags we would see hanging all around town. And she didn't tell us that she hadn't been able to find work since she'd arrived. I thought she had a job all lined up but later discovered that she only said what she needed to say to get me to her so that DSS would proceed with her funding and assistance to find housing. In order for them to continue, all of her children had to be present.

Ms. Betty was a short, thin, very petite, southern, soft spoken and religious woman. Her skin was the color of caramel and she wore a jheri curl. She was a very nice woman, until she would drink at night. She had three sons, two of whose names I can't remember. I remember one of their nicknames as Chitty and I only remember him because he was my age, seven years old at the time. They were all by different men and none of their fathers were around.

Chitty showed me all around the neighborhood, even letting me borrow his bike with the broken seat, while he ran next to me sometimes. This always reminded me of Baltimore and even in the country of the south, the hood is still the hood. We played basketball, and hide and seek. He taught me how to dig up earthworms and how to find crawfish. We would climb trees and tell each other our deepest secrets. He would tell me all about his mother, and how they ended up there in that complex. According to Chitty, Ms. Betty's parents were helping to raise them and things were going well. Ms. Betty met a man and fell in love and got married. She fell into drinking real heavy and her habit eventually destroyed her marriage and her husband left her. After that, she would curse them, her children, and blame them for HER downfall. I would tell him about Baltimore and the Party House and my family.

That first week in South Carolina, we spent about three or four of those days walking to DSS, which was about two miles away from Ms. Betty's. It was during this time that I developed a skin rash, sore throat and itchy eyes. Mommy found out it was something called Scarlet Fever, a childhood illness caused by extreme temperature changes. Leaving Baltimore, the temperature was a nice, cool, seventy-two degrees. Adjusting to the south's temperatures of nearly one hundred degrees with high humidity and dense air quality was shocking on my body. Luckily, Mommy walked me to the hospital in enough time to avoid the convulsions caused by the disease, and avoiding any permanent damage. I was sent home a few days later, and it was enough time to recover. I didn't want to miss the big day at a new school.

The night before school made me so nervous in this new place. I was so unsure and feeling uneasy about this new town, these new people, this new school. I sang the Barney song to Shay before she fell asleep that night. Feeling anxious, I even caught myself enjoying the tape, although I had seen it a thousand times. Because it was the end of the summer, Ms. Betty even saw fit to have some of the neighbors over to "shoot the shit" over a few beers. Everything was fine that night, until I heard screaming from downstairs. A slurred southern accent that I knew all too well. It was Ms. Betty. And she was screaming at her oldest son.

"Get yo dumb ass upstairs, Chitty!!!" she shrieked. "I ain't got no time for yo foolishness in here tonight! You hear me lil bitch," she slurred.

I ran to our bedroom door and cracked it open, hoping he would see me, so I could gesture him back to his room, where I could tell him to just let them be for the night. I stood there long enough to hear him stand up to her. Long enough to hear her curse him. Long enough to hear the roar of laughter from the other parents downstairs. All of this started because a drunken Ms. Betty wanted Chitty to do some type of impressions for her friends and he didn't want to, but she kept pushing. She wanted him to wake the other kids for whatever reason and when he didn't, the more upset she became. Chitty kept telling her to calm down and she shouldn't be drinking and that was the breaking point. Chitty was the one who had to get the other kids up and ready for school the following morning and he just wanted to go to bed. Then I finally realized exactly where I was; "The Party House", I mumbled to myself. I watched as Chitty screamed at his mother, who didn't even know who he was anymore. Chitty had changed when we moved in. Because Mommy was clean and doing well, that gave him the courage to stand up to his mother. When I realized that I could do no more, I closed my door, climbed back on the bedspread with a sleeping Shay. I laid on the bed and watched my young self, whom I left standing there, go hoarse screaming in the hallway.

School started. New kids. New curriculum. New teachers. New faces and rules, and circumstances at home. Mommy started going to church three nights a week, really taking her faith seriously. Her being clean and sober meant homework help each night, the occasional trip to the ice cream truck, and she even found a part time job working at Dollar General. It was like she was back to herself, back to the Mommy I wanted. She was back to being thoughtful and intuitive. If I mentioned there was some candy I wanted, even if it were a few weeks back, she would remember and surprise me with it. Just like before. But not everybody was happy to see our success. Ms. Betty would be very negative and make comments about how it wouldn't last long and when Mommy would help the kids with their homework, Ms. Betty would say negative things like her kids didn't listen. It was hard to celebrate Mommy's progress in that environment. Ms. Betty became belligerent, drinking each night, passing out at neighbors' houses, not coming home. She was a real piece of work. Ms. Betty would get so drunk that she would forget to feed her kids. She would leave the house randomly. She never helped them with homework. She treated them like they weren't important. I hated that. My mother became their helper, she would make us all hot dogs and beans and tell us stories from the Bible. She would smile at us and watch us play. Mommy was waiting for our Section 8 voucher to come through so we could finally relocate and every night, for almost a month, she was there for all of us.

Until she told us one night that we could not stay there anymore, because Ms. Betty had started using drugs.

I had never heard of Ms. Betty smoking crack but she started. And Mommy couldn't be around that. She had been clean for months and she didn't want to go back.

As hard as it was, I had to leave my surrogate brothers behind, whose names I still don't remember, except Chitty. It was an October evening while the sun was setting, where we said our goodbyes. Teary eyed goodbyes and the sting from of a jaw full of sunflower seeds in my mouth. One of the church members came to pick us up and I felt my chest tightening as the car pulled away from that house and those memories.

I was enrolled into three different schools in one month, as the three of us bounced from couch to couch with different church members, or sponsors of my mother from the NA meetings. Those times were a blur. I remember staying with one lady who was a sponsor and things were good, until she relapsed. Then we stayed with a man from her NA group and we were to stay there until housing came through, but he was on Mommy's heels and she didn't want a relationship with him so we moved on. There were times where I ate dinner at so many different places that I never even cared what town, or street we were on. I would lay in the bed, or on the floor, or the couch, and think of my grandmother, what she was doing, if she could feel me, and if I was still important to her. I wondered if she had forgotten all about me and my little sister. I would try to remember what Baltimore, my home, smelled like, and what I left behind. I learned how to cry without tears that October.

Chapter 8

The call came in November.

The call we were waiting for; the call from housing that said they finally found us a place for us to call our own. The next day my mother walked Shelae, me and our trash bags of clothes to the DSS office, where we were allowed to get our keys to our own trailer! Our trailer was in a small town called North, South Carolina. We lived on a dirt road off of another dirt road, with little sophistication and barely even telephone poles.

Our social worker, Ms. Ruby, drove us all the way there; past all the woods, past the Walmart, past the Piggly Wiggly, past the town. Our trailer sat in the middle of a ten acre clearing, a beautiful pasture with a watermelon patch behind it. We were told to stay away from the only other trailer in sight, our neighbors.

"They are some redneck ass hillbillies over yonder. Not the kind of folk y'all are use to," said Ms. Ruby. And I believed her. I was so happy to see my mother turn the key to our new place. Ms. Ruby did the best that she could with giving us a tour of the new place.

"Devin, this is gonna be your room. See, you and Shay are boy and girl, so you can't share no room!" She boasted. I was so happy to finally have a room all my own that I couldn't understand anything else she was saying. My mother, of course cried, and cried, thanking God every few minutes, shouting "In Jesus' name!" Shay and I had finally made it to the place we were promised. A place where we belonged. And Mommy was there, she had made it too. We made it together. We made it. We made it!

WE. MADE. IT.

And there we slept. No furniture. Not an old chair. Not an old sofa. Absolutely nothing. Except an old refrigerator that made a screeching noise almost every hour on the hour. With a half-eaten bucket of chicken from KFC, a mound of blankets and our trash bags of clothes, we all finally found our peace. The kind of peace that allows for good sleep, with deep dreams. We all held each other tight, smiling, crying and sniffling throughout that November night.

It was only a matter of time before we made our house a home. Ms. Ruby took a liking to my mother, even making sure that she had a ride to weekend meetings thirty miles away. She gave us Good Will vouchers for furniture, food stamps for food, and even cleaning supplies. She got me enrolled into North Elementary School and helped us to get a fresh start in a small town where NOBODY knew us. This remote location of our trailer meant venturing out into the surrounding woods a lot by myself, seeing animals and birds that I'd never seen before.

Watching the moonlight in the tub through the bathroom window made me feel calm at night. Our trailer was full of love. We ate dinner with each other every night. Mommy laughed at all of my jokes and we were trying to teach Shay to talk. Perfect nights. I spent most of those days wandering through the woods, talking to God, thanking Him for helping us. Wondering if we would stay this happy forever.

Taking out the trash one afternoon in my bare feet, a small black, spotted puppy ran to my feet, and began licking my toes. I reached down for the small pup, feeling him shake in the fall air.

"Get on back up here now, Pup!"

I looked up to my neighbor's trailer where the voice came from and there stood a white kid, a little taller than me, stocky build, long golden blonde, curly hair, with a voice like he'd been here before. He sounded like a very old, wise, country, southern gentleman. I remembered what Ms. Ruby said, and reached for my back door knob to go inside. I didn't want no trouble.

"He ain't gon' bite ya none, he just wan' play a lil bit," he snorted.

"Wh-what's your name??" I asked.

"Mike," he said. We shook hands. He told me that his dog had recently had a litter of puppies and that this one loved to run and play. He laughed, and so did I.

"What's yo name then, buddy?" He asked.

"Devin." I said boastfully.

"Well, you comin' out tomorrow? We can gon' down to ride bikes," he said.

I nodded my head 'yes' and watched them walk away. I didn't know how much this friend I had just made, the one Ms. Ruby told me to stay away from, would mold my young life in the south.

***

"Well, damn, Buddy, gon' and kill it already!!" screamed a frustrated Michael.

It was a cold Saturday in January, and Mike was in Phase Two of teaching me how to hunt squirrels. Phase One was with Mike showing me how to hold the gun and telling me how I had to squint my eyes to get a better look. We were using his brand-new rifle, a BB gun from Christmas, a fancy Winchester with a heavy barrel. It's the only thing he'd asked for. Mike had no problem killing any animal in those woods. His green eyes fixated on any life that dared move when we were out there. "Adventure huntin" is what he called it. Mike's older brothers were typical redneck teens with beat-up old pick up trucks that they drove through the seasons. That's who showed him how to shoot so good. They loved Mike. And I think, over time, that they'd even grown to love me a little. Which was weird in our little area.

Mike's mother was a woman named Ms. Geraldine, a tall, thin woman with no bottom teeth. She didn't believe in shoes, and walked barefoot for every single day that I'd known her. She had a strong face, a face that showed her Native American heritage. She also had a look that was cold and hard. I didn't know what she'd been through, but you could see that she's been through some hard times. She looked like a true hillbilly. Her boys were all she had. And she was all they had. Sometimes when me and Mike would hunt, he would tell me stories of his father, or "Diddy" as he called him. I could tell that they all missed him being around, but I never had the courage to ask what had happened to him.

"SHOOT! Boy, KILL 'em!!!'" Mike screamed. I pulled the trigger the way he'd shown me, missing the squirrel who was now running up the mangled oak tree for cover. I squeezed the trigger again, and again and again.

"Hot damn, there boy!! I thank we don' found dinna!" Mike shouted.

I finally opened my eyes to find the furry squirrel down. I had done it. Me! I finally did it! The squirrel felt warm when I finally touched him with my bare hand. His

eyes still partially opened creeped me out. While Michael

was running all around me singing some type of indian

chant, I grabbed for my gloves and started heading back

toward the house. I could hear Ms. Geraldine's voice

echoing through the woods.

"Mi-cheal!!! Dev-in!!!!"

We twisted our bodies through the mangled bushes

and vines to get through to the clearing where we saw the

tiny figures standing, which were our mothers standing so

far away. I started to realize how cold my body was when

we started walking through the frozen field. As we inched

closer to the trailers, Michael was telling this elaborate

hoax of a tale from when he killed three black bears in the

woods. I laughed at Mike, while glaring down at the

squirrel in my right hand, all the while thinking of the boy

that got hit by the car back in Baltimore. I couldn't

remember his name, but I remember how it made me feel. That boy lay there bloody, motionless, just like the squirrel.

"Is this the same thing?" I mumbled to myself.

I watched my mother get closer, and I felt the guilt come on harder with each step that I took. Mike was proud, yet, I was sad. What was wrong with me?

"I know that you heard us callin' you!" My mother shouted. I didn't realize how cold I was inside until I stopped walking, noticing the blood trail from our squirrel carcasses.

"Me and Devin wanna cook these for dinner tonight Momma!!" Mike said.

"They is wild animals Michael, and I ain't puttin' them squirrels in no pots of mine!" Ms. Geraldine shouted.

Mommy and I laughed at them as we pushed open the screen door to the porch of our house and we all sat down trying to get warm again while Mommy made us some tea. Mike began telling our mothers the "Bear Story" while I sat indian style in front of the door. Even after

finally getting warm, I still felt cold and numb inside.

Chapter 9

Things were finally going well. The past winter had bought me a best friend, Shay a few more teeth, and Mommy a new boyfriend.

Mike and I had become inseperable. I helped him feed the dogs everyday and he even gave Shay and me a puppy for helping out. We would take nature walks through different parts of our area. I would tell him about Baltimore and all about my family, mostly about my grandmother. I would tell him about the library, and how drugs changed the landscape of an entire city. Mike couldn't grasp the concept of a busy city, where people wore shoes EVERYDAY and where people would drive cars too fast and listen to their music too loud. Almost everyday, I tried to explain the details that I remembered to him. This helped me to never forget where I came from.

Mike and I would ride bikes forever, barefoot sometimes, even making "dirt jumps" in the middle of the road. We made trails and caught lightening bugs. We would climb trees and sing silly songs on the bus ride home. We would get dirty, chase deer, and shoot at birds that were too far away to hit. We would build paper planes and have flying contests. We would get mad at each other in the morning, and shoot off his older brother's fireworks by the afternoon. He acted like my opinion mattered.

Like I was important.

This silver tooth wearing, barefoot, redneck was my brother.

Chapter 10

"I know you did great again! That's my baby! I'm telling y'all, my son is one of the smartest kids y'all ever gon' meet. You know he won a reading contest back in Bal-more, right?" My mother stammered as she'd started drinking again. She spoke from a slurred mouth to her friends one late Saturday night. It was late in the spring, almost summer, which meant report cards were coming out. I knew that I had great grades, so I loved this time of the school year.

Mommy's boyfriend, JB, had started staying with us almost every weekend. He was a tall, dark skinned, bald headed southern man. He worked hard, and also had a family with a girlfriend and children somewhere in the city.

-Michaels Interlude (The Honor Roll story)

"I heard that it all started from a good thing. Devin's mother had developed a relationship with a South Carolina man named JB. JB worked as a labourer and made good money. JB would always come through to their trailer towards the end of the week, bearing gifts, food, and drugs for Ms. Dorray. I'm only telling you all of this because I know that Devin would never feel comfortable telling it. He never is.

Devin was always smart in school, way more than me. JB promised Ms. Dorray and Devin that if he was able to get on the honor roll at the end of the school year, that he would treat them to a weekend getaway, someplace where they could have some fun. Weeks later, the end of the school year came, and of course, Devin was on the honor roll, earning all "A's" and one "B". JB kept his word, and asked Devin where it was that he wanted to go. Devin told me that he always wanted to go to the Go Kart Track at the amusement park outside of North. All of us kids heard about the brand-new track and wanted to eventually see what all the hype was all about. Devin even came to my house to brag about the trip before they all piled up in JB's Cutlass. I was so happy for him. He told me that they arrived shortly after seven on that Saturday night. Too late to get to the track, JB found them a hotel for the night. It was the kind of place that really was two rooms in one, with one of those doors in the middle to connect the rooms. He and a one-year old Shay shared a room. They ate KFC that night, and were exhausted from the long day. Ms. Dorray and JB stayed in the other room for the entire time, smoking crack rocks.

Some time in the middle of the night, he said that the door opened. The only light in the small room was from the t.v. Devin pretended to be sleep, to play a trick on his mother. He heard her walking over to the side of the bed that Shay was on. He peeked through the covers to find that, instead of Ms. Dorray tucking Shay in, it was JB! What was JB doing in their room? JB looked nervous and fidgety. Devin said he knew that something wasn't right, so he coughed. He coughed loud enough for JB to be rattled away from Shay and move out of the room. Only he never left the room, he came over to his side of the bed.

Devin told me that he could smell the smoke in his clothes as he felt JB's hands slide through the sheets. He pulled down Devin's pajama pants, feeling him up and down all over his private parts. Devin said he kept wondering what was JB doing and why was he doing this? Did he lose his mind? Was this normal? Should he fight him off? Should he just lay there? And where was his mother?

It's a bunch of stuff that he did to my friend before he eventually pulled his own pants down, almost in an attempt to get into the bed, before hearing muffled noises from the other room. Then JB left. And then it was over. Devin told me that he lay there awake staring at Shay sleep until the sun came up. He said he felt disgusting. And in pain. He felt like he wasn't important. I wish that I could've been there for him. I hate that I couldn't, because the boy had been through enough. Don't ever tell him where you heard this from. Don't tell him how I told you this. Selling my old buddy out for a story, humph. Hope it's worth it."

Chapter 11

I tried to think of how to tell her. Bouncing around in the back seat of JB's car made me feel nauseous that entire ride home. Shay wanting to play and make silly faces was normally a fun time but now, it annoyed me. JB and Mommy listened to the radio, so loud that I couldn't complete my thoughts. That annoyed me. We drove for an hour to get back to the trailer. We finally pulled into the grass in front of our house as the sun was setting. When JB ran to the house to use the bathroom, I told Mommy.

"Mommy, I gotta tell you about something that happened". Mommy looked back with a happy face.

"What's going on, Dev?" I tried my hardest to tell her what happened as fast as I could, before he could get back, and so I didn't have to feel embarrassed. I was so nervous to tell Mommy how nasty I felt. I wanted to take a bath, and wash away the weekend. I knew that she would be surprised, and I knew that she would be mad at him. I knew that she would be upset to have to lose what she thought was a "good man". But she was Mommy. My superwoman. My friend. My rock. And that's just what needed to be done.

Or maybe not.

Mommy's face went from happy to puzzled, like she was surprised about something.

"Wait, wait Devin, what you mean? JB wouldn't do no shit like that. Are you sure you weren't dreaming?"

Dreaming. Dreaming? Are you kidding me? Mommy told me to shut up, and to get outta the car. She told me to keep my voice down, and to stop imagining things. I felt numb as JB came back to the car. Numb. I could see them talking and laughing. Not a care in the world for her. Like I didn't just tell her what happened.

I stared at the faucet real hard that night in the bathtub. The same bathtub that was so pretty to me when we first moved in. I searched my mind for the last song I heard on the radio. I searched my mind for my grandmother, and what she would think about me now, her grandson not even a boy anymore. Was I really a boy still? I didn't feel like a boy. Was I a girl? I didn't feel like a girl. I didn't feel like a child or a man. I felt lost and helpless. I felt weak. I didn't feel whole. I felt confused. A man isn't supposed to do that to a guy. So what did that make me? I scrubbed my skin with the small bar of soap, jealous of the bubbles that the washcloth left behind. If I could transform into the bubbles, I would have. The bubbles served a simple purpose. The perfectly round bubbles only served to provide comfort and cleanliness. I still felt dirty though. Mommy didn't bring me a towel that night like she always did, and my room was a little cold. Through the vents, I heard her moans.

Her forgetting what I said.

Her forgetting what was important.

Nothing was the same after the sun set that day. The ants still came through the cracks in the door. The puppies still ran for feeding time. My sister still laughed at the planes that I made out of her little spoon. My mother still moaned through the vents. And my family was still too far away to hear me. Everything was the same, yet, everything was different.

Summer came fast that year. The school year was good but I was mostly quiet. When June rolled around, Mimi and Pop Pop were coming down to get Shay and me for the entire summer, and I couldn't wait to see them. That meant riding back to Baltimore, back to my roots, and back to my family.

I vowed to learned how to punt a football that summer. So barefoot and silly, I was out in the front yard practicing my "field goal attempts" in an imaginary goal post. I heard a small shudder from a far away truck. A truck riding faster than usual for our dirt road. I noticed the blue Ford as it gleamed past our old mailbox at the dirt heap. It was Pop Pop! I nearly jumped out of my skin when I saw my grandmother's curls bouncing in the passenger seat. I felt excited, for the first time, in a long time. My grandmother's smile made my eyes swell with tears before the truck even stopped. She wore dark aviator sunglasses and an early tan. And she was really here. Pop Pop pulled onto the grass and turned the truck off. I don't know who said "hello" first and I didn't care. They were here! I ran to Mimi and grabbed her jeans as I held onto her legs and cried in happiness on her shoulder when she picked me up. I cried until I couldn't breathe anymore. I told her how much I missed her, and couldn't wait to leave. I ran to Pop Pop, and cried on his shoulder too. He picked me up, letting my legs swing. His mustache tickled my cheek, and I felt his tears on my cheek. I missed them so much, and I knew they missed me. I felt complete again. I felt whole.

I felt important.

We rode back to Baltimore for eight hours. I sat in the back of the pickup, staring at the aftermarket roof. Completely content. Free of fears. Pop Pop stopped to get us snacks for the road, our eyes catching each other's ever so often before the sun finally set. Shay sat in the front with Mimi. Before we left, Mommy tried to act like she wasn't hungover from the night before, like Mimi didn't know any better. She asked Mimi why she didn't call and Mimi reminded her that the phone was off. Without even packing bags for us, we left with just the clothes on our backs. The ride home felt like an escape, but only a partial escape. I felt like a piece of me was still there. Like the old me was in Baltimore, but this new me, the one who was still in that hotel room, was still in the south.

Pop Pop woke me up as we got off the last exit on I-295 heading into Baltimore City. It felt so good to be back home, but not like I expected. The city seemed dirtier than I remembered. It was just- different. Or maybe it wasn't Baltimore that was different; maybe it was me.

Mimi explained that Shay and I would be spending the summer between her house and Aunt Monica & Aunt Ava's new duplex. The first day back, I felt normal again, playing in the back alley of Mimi's house, with my old shoes and toys that were still there. I told all of my friends on Coldspring Lane about Mike back in South Carolina, and the woods, the puppies, and the watermelon patch. I told them about how incredibly quiet it was in the country, and the bright green grass and open fields. I told them how people actually drive dirty pick up trucks and walk around barefoot. They couldn't believe that places like that even existed, as most of them had never left the city limits. All of the family was so excited to see Shay and me after so much time passed. We played with cousins, met with aunts, and caught up with people I didn't remember from before. Some time after that, we ended up at the duplex apartment

Aunt Monica and Aunt Ava shared. They were so happy to see us. Aunt Monica had a daughter, Temia, that was the same age as Shay. I was there when Temia was born, and she was excited to have us there for the summer. The first night, Aunt Ava made her signature potato salad, fried fish and collard greens! We ate, talked about Mommy and how she was doing. They were definitely bothered when I told them that she was using again. Aunt Monica mentioned that I seemed like I didn't want to be touched at all and kept asking me what was wrong. I told her that I was just tired from the long ride home and we put the dishes away. She and Aunt Ava took me out on the front porch with them after they put the girls to sleep, just to talk, explaining to me that I could tell them anything, and that I shouldn't hesitate to tell them anything that was bothering me. Aunt Monica must have sensed that there was more to what I was telling them because she just wouldn't let up. So, after telling them all about everything EXCEPT JB, I knew that the time had come for me to share the details of the night that made me shudder with embarrassment. So, I told them everything about that night. They both cried themselves and they cried with me; Aunt Monica kissing me and apologizing to me for them not being there to save us from that. I'd never seen them cry like that before. It made me feel better getting it off my chest too, but I feared the backlash. I could tell that this wasn't something that they would just sweep under the rug, nor were they gonna let this go without telling Mimi. That night, as I prepared for bed, I knew that they were gonna make me tell Mimi, the same way that I had told it to them. A conversation that I didn't think I was built to have just yet.

It was about a week after I told Aunt Monica, on a hot afternoon, when I told her. I'm pretty sure that my aunts already told her but they wanted to give me time to tell her on my own. Mimi cried as hard as I knew that she would, when I explained to her what had taken place in

South Carolina. Every detail made her walk away shaking, even leaving her watered-down lemonade on the glider that lived on her brick porch. Mimi explained to me that what happened to me wasn't right, as she held me and kissed my cheeks. She apologized for that day, vowing to make it right. After a tearful day, we went for snowballs on Monroe Street and talked about the murders in Baltimore that year. She told me how out of control the violence had become. She liked to talk about real issues and how to solve the root of the problem and not just cover it up. Mimi hugged me for no reason at all several times that week.

Eventually, we got back into our groove. Library trips and long talks about the future. Mimi told me that I was a warrior, much like Nelson Mandela in South Africa. She told me about the sixties and how much our ancestors had found triumph in their struggles coming up in America. Mimi found a way to make me feel stronger from my experience, rather than a victim. She always asked me how

I was feeling. And what she could do to make our summer better.

She made me feel important.

She was still the same Mimi. Always Caring. Always making sure Shay and I were happy!

The summer was a blur. Visits from uncles and extended family members that reminded me of how much I had grown in the years since they'd seen us. By August, I think Mommy had called one time, finally getting to a phone. She asked how we were, and telling me how bad Mike had missed Shay and me. Shelae spent most of the summer with Temia at Aunt Monica's house. Shay and Temia became more like sisters, playing and learning together. I was so happy for her! My aunts ran their households with structure, and bed times. Shay needed that. So did I. But as we settled into routine, it was time for us to get back down south. My mother said that the new school year was coming and she wanted us back home. I just wasn't ready to go back. Baltimore was familiar. My family was here. My memories. The mommy from before was still here. Baltimore was home.

Mimi, Shay and I reached South Carolina around seven in the morning, as I woke up from a deep sleep on a pillow drenched from sweat in the backseat. Mimi asked where we wanted to stop for an early breakfast as this was the "one last stop" before heading home. I chose the local Cracker Barrel. We ate and laughed about the last batch of cookies we had brought with us; how we had to stretch the flour, and how the kitchen was a mess last night. After breakfast, we got back on the road to head home. Shay was falling back to sleep as we pulled up to the brick building with the bold letters "DSS" on the front. We walked inside, greeted by an antsy Ms. Ruby, who said she missed us, and wanted to speak to me.

Ms. Ruby spoke to me in a quiet room with toys all around. My grandmother sat upright in her chair asking me to tell Ms. Ruby about JB. She explained how this was the last time I would have to tell the story of what happened that night, in detail, to somebody else.

I sat in the corner chair, watching Mimi play with Shelae out of the corner of my eye. Ms. Ruby took notes, pausing every few moments, cupping her hands while I told her what happened. This time when I told the story, I noticed something was different. I had changed since the last time I spoke about the hotel room, JB, and that night. I replayed the events of that night so many times in my mind over the summer, that I was no longer affected, or even emotional when I thought about it. I became numb to the entire incident. Ms. Ruby looked over her glasses at me, gripping her clipboard, and asked did I want a hug, or some Kleenex. I gave her a quick "no" and told her I was ready to get back home to see how Mommy was doing. And so, after a few more moments, we were leaving. I sat in the back seat with the window down, looking over the city as we drove down those familiar roads. I saw Ms. Geraldine outside in a brown pickup truck with a cigarette hanging from her mouth as we pulled up. She hollered out for Mike as soon as she recognized that it was us that pulled up.

I bought all of the bags in as Mimi walked around the dusty trailer. It seemed so different. Just a few months ago, we all found peace here, sleeping on the floor that first night. Just the three of us. This was our new beginning. Now, this wasn't home anymore. I spent the summer in comfort and peace and surrounded by so much love. How could they bring me back here after knowing what happened to me? I didn't want to be here.

Mommy was still asleep, even though it was so late in the afternoon. We knew exactly what that meant; a night of partying. I watched a tall dark-skinned man excuse himself from her bedroom when my grandmother walked in to wake my mother. I couldn't hear everything that

Mommy was saying to Mimi, because Shay was so eager to get to her toys that were tossed all around in her room.

Mimi came into my room, asking if I had everything that we packed before leaving Baltimore. I showed her the two new pair of Nike that Pop Pop bought me for school. She smiled a half smile and walked toward me. Mimi hugged me and held onto me for a long time, reminding me to "take care of your sister," like she always said. "You're all that she has, Devin".

As only she could, Mimi looked at me like I was important. She retreated to Shay's room and whispered something in her ear before using the bathroom, and exiting our trailer. She stared at my mother, who was now on the porch smoking a cigarette, as she walked to her burgundy Cutlass. Mommy looked away, clearly hungover from yet another night of partying. Two minutes later, Mimi was turning off of the first dirt road and I watched from Shay's window, until she was out of sight. Mimi was gone.

"So how was your summer, y'all?" Mommy asked in an intoxicating tone.

"It was great." I said, not even looking in her direction. She walked over and watched Shay play for a moment with her colorful building blocks, and went in her room to go back to sleep. I wasn't happy about being here with her and she didn't seem happy to see us either. She made me feel like we were in her way. Mike ran past the window toward the front porch, with a huge bag of beef jerky, sunflower seeds, a gleam in his eye, and a summer's worth of exploring to tell me all about. I snapped back into reality when my best friend swung the rickety trailer door open. We. Were. Back. Home.

If it could even be called one.

***

School started on a muggy September morning, right after Labor Day. I was so excited to show off my new shoes and clothes that Pop Pop had bought me just two weeks prior. I couldn't wait to tell all of the kids on the bus all about the big city and how I'd gone back to visit for the summer. Of course, I would embellish just a wee bit about the friends I had back in Baltimore. I found it amazing how naive they all were. They would believe anything I told them. I over exaggerated a little, sometimes, but I never lied to them. I met my teachers, and even the young lady that Mike had been talking about all summer from our school. Mommy called a couple of times from Mike's phone and I got to speak to him during those times. All he talked about was this girl and I couldn't wait to find out who she was. One of my classmates, Logan Barr, was very happy to see me. He said that he'd dropped by the trailer over the summer, to invite me to his birthday party, but nobody ever answered the door. Logan was a cool kid. He and I had worked on a science project the previous spring that earned us both an A in the class. His dark brown hair matched his freckles and his big, brown, puppy eyes. He wore his hair spiky, and was very popular. His father came to our school a lot, as he was a volunteer fire fighter and always explaining to children the importance of smoke detectors in the home. On the way home from school, Logan sat next to me on the bus. We talked and laughed of our summer experiences. At some point, I felt lost in the many names of his friends that he mentioned, and the places he and his family visited over the summer. I watched his mouth move as I imagined how he would react to what happened to me that night in the hotel room. He'd knew nothing of the struggles of my life. He knew nothing of having a drug addicted mother. He knew nothing of having to look after a younger sister. He knew nothing of losing your identity in a hotel room. His whole life was planned out. After all, he was white. And rich.

"See, right there is my house man!" He pointed to the biggest ranch I'd ever seen, through the cloudy school bus window.

"That's it? That's your house?" I asked.

"Yup! Hopefully you'll come over this weekend!" He shouted. He slapped the bus driver a high five, as he went trotting down his long driveway toward the behemoth of a home.

Logan's home couldn't be described as anything less than huge. By the size, you would think that a professional athlete would live there. It was a brick structure with big windows on the first floor. The first time I spent the night there, was purely by accident. Logan had a birthday party at a Go Kart track and when his mother took me home, no one was home at my house. So, his mother figured that since my mother had their phone number, I could just sleep over and Mommy would call later. I knew she wouldn't but I didn't want to tell Logan's mother that. I walked into

Logan's house and the ceiling was endless! The house was bigger on the inside than any other house I'd ever seen. His house had six bedrooms and I lost count of how many bathrooms. The property was huge and you could ride go karts along the makeshift course that was on their property. There was a horse stable and three horses! The only time I'd ever seen a horse was on the streets of Baltimore and there was always a cop sitting on top.

Logan had the perfect life. Not because of the house he lived in, but because of his family. His dad was a volunteer firefighter but I think he made his living as some sort of lawyer. His mom was a stay at home mom, but not because of drugs or anything. She stayed at home because she wanted to. She played dress up with Logan's baby sister and they sang songs together. His mother treated me like I was one of their own. I always felt welcome at Logan's house and never wanted to leave. I had dreams of being adopted by them and living in their house and having family time. They didn't worry about what they would have for dinner or what activities they wanted to do. Their lives seemed so carefree and fun. I had never seen parents interact the way they did. They were loving and affectionate towards each other. They seemed to like each other. They seemed happy.

Logan taught me how to ride a horse. I was scared at first but Logan had a way of talking you through your fears. He made you feel that there was no difference between him and you regardless of what the outside looked like or what the world said. Logan made me feel like the world was alright.

After Logan got off the bus, I could feel heavy breathing on my neck as the bus pulled away. I turned around to see a dirty faced Mike with a dandelion, half blown, wedged between his teeth.

"I go to talk to my girl for awhile, and you go givin' my seat to a snobby," he snorted.

I turned away from him snickering, looking out onto the watermelon patch that sat behind our homes which looked nothing like Logan's. We raced to our trailers as we always did, Mike making me promise to come out and ride bikes after homework. I ran inside calling for Mommy and Shay, and not getting an answer, I figured she'd found a ride to the grocery store in town. I ran to the refrigerator and scoffed down the last of the orange juice from days ago, pulling off my backpack. I figured I had better get started with my homework so I could go riding with Mike, but after homework, I wanted to write Mimi a letter to let her know how the first day of school went and how Shay and I were doing. I had forgotten all about the stamps that she'd mailed out to me, strictly for this reason. She wanted me to write as many letters as I wanted. I climbed into my closet, digging for the stamps that I kept in a backpack. This backpack held a lot of my pictures and toys and little memories that I brought back with me from Baltimore.

Upon finding them, I noticed my Nike shoebox was on the floor, near my play clothes and baseball glove. I knew that I'd never leave my new shoes here. My school shoes stayed at the top of the closet, in the box. Always. Then it dawned on me. I knew exactly what happened. Mommy happened. I opened the empty box. She sold my shoes. She waited until the first day of school, when I wouldn't be at home to guard them, and sold my white Nike Airs that Pop Pop had bought for me. That's why she wasn't home. I flopped on the carpet in disgust staring blankly into the closet. My mind, my heart, and my thoughts, were stuck in a thick haze of confusion, anger, and the reality of what happened.

Chapter 12

"Devin, you do know how long two weeks is, right?" Ms. Ruby asked me for a second time. I heard her the first time, but I didn't bother answering her. I was too busy watching the squirrel run up and down the tree outside of her rain covered office window.

"That's fourteen days, Ms. Ruby." I answered her.

"Yes, indeed it is Devin, are you ready?"

Again, I didn't answer as I looked back out the window, searching for my squirrel friend, who I imagined could come and trade places with me if I stared at him hard enough. The two weeks she was referring to, was the amount of time before Shay and I went into foster care. In the last month, we'd found out that the day that my grandmother took me to DSS to tell Ms. Ruby about what happened with JB, I was being recorded on a closed-circuit camera. In the state of South Carolina, such a recording could be used as evidence for the state, to be used against my mother, proving negligence, and her not being of proper mental health to raise her two young children. I was angry at Mimi. She tricked me into telling on my mother. I knew that her reasons for doing so came from a good place, but I didn't care. Now, Shay and I were going to a strange place to live, forever.

It was during this time that I discovered that when Mimi took me to DSS, she herself was hoping to get temporary custody of me and Shay. She wanted us to go back to Baltimore and live with her. She was told, by her mother who was a Baltimore City social worker, that once DSS found out and did their investigation, if it was determined that we needed to be removed from my mother's custody, DSS would contact her and then we would be placed in her custody. So, this is the impression that Mimi had when we walked into DSS on that day. She didn't realize that the laws are different in each state. Maryland's foster care system is largely overcrowded so if this incident happened in Maryland, they would have called Mimi and we would have been placed in her care. South Carolina law is different. South Carolina law states that if the children need to be removed from the mother's custody, they are to be placed into the foster care system first, regardless if there is a family member willing to care for the children. Mimi thought she was helping and we would be with her, but instead, things got worse and we would be going to live with strangers.

I sat in the backseat with my mother and Shay, feeling numb, while Mariah Carey's "Hero" blared through the radio. I could sense my mother's hatred towards Ms. Ruby, as she opted to sit in the back with us, instead of sitting next to Ms. Ruby. She had already cursed me out last week, saying that I'm stupid for "running my mouth to those damn people".

I felt so many emotions at the same time, that I just drifted from school to home. I was just going through the motions. It was too much for me. Shay was asleep on Mommy's shoulder as she slammed Ms. Ruby's car door upon exiting. Ms. Ruby looked over her glasses at me as I was getting out.

"Devin, are you ok?" She asked in a low tone.

"Yup, I'm fine." I slammed her door and didn't look back, stomping through the mud puddles leading to our trailer steps. I stared directly into the rain as the Chevy Cavalier, one of the many company cars for Ms. Ruby, pulled off, wanting to scream into the emptiness that I felt within.

I didn't fully understand what was actually about to happen. Mommy was pissed at me when Ms. Ruby left. I mean, she was really angry. She didn't speak to me or cook dinner that night. I thought she would be mad and maybe we'd have to go to some counseling or therapy of some sort. I thought that foster care would be like going someplace on the weekends while Mommy went to meetings or something. I thought it was just a way of helping us get back on track. Mommy even had company that night and, the next day, she was talking to me again as if nothing happened. She never spoke to me about anything. I thought things would be alright. I didn't know the full extent of what was happening until those fourteen days were up and Ms. Ruby was at the house again.

Chapter 13

"Devin, did you tell your friends goodbye?" Asked a hungover Mommy from the kitchen breakfast bar.

"Yeah, I told them," I replied. I stood in the living room, staring out of the front window into the grassy acre that was our front yard. Today was the day. The last day. I tried to imagine how it would be when Ms. Ruby pulled up. I turned around to the empty spot that WAS our television in the living room. Mommy sold it a few days ago during the week while I was in school. It was the last television set that we owned. The house was very quiet that afternoon. Shay wasn't even awake yet, and it was one o'clock in the afternoon. It was almost like she could feel that today was the last day that we would be there. I jumped when I heard the front door slam, when Mike came in breathing heavy. He didn't say anything as he entered, just glaring at

Mommy with a mean look on his face. He came close and whispered to me.

"Hey, Devin, I got a idea."

I didn't say anything; I just grabbed my jacket and ran for the front door. We both walked past the bags that were neatly packed by the front door and stepped out into the crisp October air. A dark gray Oldsmobile pulled up, with a mangled front bumper. It was one of Mommy's "friends". He threw up a hand to say hello as he was pulling something from the car. Mike and I both acted as if we didn't see him, as we started to walk to his house.

"We can just hide you and Shay here," Mike finally said in a soft whisper. "Yeah, you and Shay are just gonna hide here in the crawl space. Momma ain't gon' say nothin'."

I forced a smile on my face as I knew exactly what my best friend meant. He didn't want me to leave, just as bad as I wasn't ready to leave. We sat on his back porch in total silence after that, for a good while, watching the puppies run all around after each other near the edge of the watermelon patch. Mike's house was quiet too. We both jumped when his older brother, Jeremy, came outside the back door to the mobile home. He looked at both of us, and started doing some impromptu karate moves on us- playing around trying to lighten the mood. We both laughed at him, and "fought back". He got down on one dirty knee, and hugged me. Ol' Jeremy, the same redneck that refused to even speak to me or my mother when we first moved in, was crying, all because he knew that I was leaving. I cried too. Mike came over and put his arms around the both of us. And he cried.

"Now, you know you always got a home here with us. Don't ya?" he said.

"Yeah I know, Jeremy, and thanks for teaching me how to change oil." I said while drying my face. Jeremy smirked and used his T-shirt to wipe away his tears. He lit a cigarette and walked off towards the clearing that sat between both of our houses. Mike and I followed the puppies around front, where Ms. Geraldine was sipping what appeared to be lemonade out of an old mason jar. As soon as she saw us, she began to cry. When I started walking towards her, she put her hands up, as if to say "I can't deal with this right now". She lit a cigarette, and walked into the house. Mike and I sat on the edge of his porch, still not saying one word to each other. I smelled the all too familiar smell of their house escape in the light breeze that passed. I closed my eyes and thought about how many nights and days that woman fed Shay and me at that small dining room table; how many nights we fell asleep watching Roseanne, waiting for Mommy to get back, or to wake up, or to be done with her "company". Before I knew it, another car was pulling down our dirt road. It was Ms. Ruby. She pulled the navy-blue Chrysler down next to the Oldsmobile that was already parked in our grass. I was hoping it wasn't her because the car was different from the last time. But the license tag indicated it was a state car so I knew it was her.

She waved at Jeremy who was leaning on the corner of our trailer. Jeremy spit toward her car, and walked away.

"Hey Devin, you all about ready? Where's Dorray?" Ms. Ruby asked.

"She inside." Jeremy scoffed.

I walked slowly towards the house, Mike two steps behind me, sulking with each step. Mommy stood near the door, getting Shelae's jacket on, while she was finally waking up. Mommy stood to give Ms. Ruby a hug, and began crying. Ms. Ruby whispered something in her ear, and it made mommy cry even harder. Mommy's friend was still in the bedroom. She hadn't even asked him to leave so we could have this private moment.

"Temporary, Dorray. This is just temporary. They're gonna be fine." Ms. Ruby said, wiping her own tears from under her glasses.

Mike and I grabbed the trash bags full of our clothes, and filled the trunk to Ms. Ruby's car with them. Ms. Ruby already had a car seat for Shay in the backseat. Mommy hugged Shay as she loaded her into the car. She laughed at Mommy, thinking that it was play time, confused at what was happening. Mommy fought back tears when she came around the back of the car to hug me. While she was holding me, I couldn't cry. I simply couldn't feel anything for her at that moment. I had seen her cry so many times and she never did anything to keep this from happening. She didn't even believe me when I told her what happened with JB. She told me I was dreaming and making up things. Mommy had company over right now. Once we left, she would go back to getting high and living her life, the only difference being was me and Shay wouldn't be there. I saw

Ms. Geraldine sobbing deeply in her yard with Jeremy holding her as her body went limp in his arms.

"Take care of your sister, you hear? This is all just temporary. Mommy gotta get herself together." Mommy whimpered out.

"I know, Ma" I replied. I held her again, and could feel the reality beginning to set in for all of us. We were really leaving to go live somewhere else because she didn't want to believe me. Shay held her hand out for me in the backseat, as I climbed in. Ms. Ruby handed Mommy some papers while Mike came to the window and hugged me.

"I wish we could just run away," He said, tears streaming from both eyes.

"Me too, brother." I said looking away. I felt my chest tighten as Ms. Ruby started the car. Mommy ran to the window, digging in her pockets, and handed me a five dollar bill and seven one dollar bills. That must've been everything that she had to her name. I cried when we locked eyes for what I knew, in my heart, would be the last time.

"Momma." Shay whispered while gripping my hand hard. She looked so confused as to what was going on, while Mommy walked away from the car. The car did a full circle turn to go out of the grass and back to the dirt road when I saw Mommy's face reappear on the front porch. She was screaming something as she ran towards the car.

"Ms. RUBAY!! Ms. Rubbay!" She shouted. Ms. Ruby slowed the car down, as she slipped the wooden picture frame into my window.

"Hold on to this always, Devin! I love y'all. Please take care of your sister!" She panted.

She looked me right in the eyes and said, "No matter how far away we are, remember that we are always under the same sky!"

I became hysterical. "I love you, Mommy." I whispered.

"Find the stars whenever you miss me, baby!" She cried. Mommy backed away from the window, and Ms. Ruby pulled off slowly. I turned around in my seat and watched her fall in the grass, Ms. Geraldine ran over to her just as we turned the final corner onto the main dirt road. I wiped the tears away as fast as I could to remember the scene; every tree, the mailbox, the bushes and shrubs, Ms. Geraldine, Michael, Jeremy. I knew in my heart that life would never be the same again for Shay and me. The pain turned into fear, just as I turned around, looking at the picture I was holding in my hand. It was the picture we had taken last Christmas. Mommy held Shay in her lap, and I stood next to Mommy with my arm on her shoulder. We all smiled hard. Genuine happiness. One of the best days in my life was captured in that picture. As I held that best day in my hand, one of the worst days in my life was in my reality. I stared at the smiles in the picture until my eyes grew too weak to stay open. Shay smiled at me as I fell asleep, as she, too, went back to sleep. Ms. Ruby turned the radio on, and adjusted the mirror to look at us.

"No matter how far away we are," I repeated. "No matter how far."

Chapter 14

We woke up in a Burger King parking lot. The cartoon characters bright and vibrant on the windows. Ms. Ruby's hands were cold as she touched me to wake me up. I felt groggy and exhausted, like when Mommy had given me cold medicine when I was sick before bed.

"Come on, Dev, you wanna get something to eat?" Ms. Ruby said. She was already holding Shay in her arms while I climbed out of the back seat.

"Please don't call me that. Only my family calls me that at home." I said, in a low tone.

"What? Dev?" She asked. I nodded as we walked into Burger King. The realities of the day were coming back to me as we stood in the lobby before ordering. Ms. Ruby asked the cashier for two cheeseburger kids meals, and pointed at the crowns they had sitting on the counter.

She motioned for me to get one, but I wasn't feeling like a "King" at all. I watched her out the corner of my eye, as she prepared the table, sitting Shay in one of the metal high chairs. I slowly walked to the table, staring at the plastic cling-ons of the Kids Club characters they had on the windows. There was a black character, that looked like he was an athlete. His name was Jaws. He had a subtle smile, and wore a green sweatshirt and blue shorts. I stared at his smile, and for a moment, I closed my eyes. I wondered that if I wished hard enough, at just that second, if I could become a character too, forever frozen in time in the picture with him. Maybe I could be the character "D", with a smile just like Jaws' and I could live in their world, and that this whole day would just be a twisted dream to me. I would look out from the picture I was in, at the child that stood in front of the picture. Maybe my super-power would be the ability to be able to save souls, and to change the past for kids.

"Dev- - I mean, Dev-in, sit down, honey, and eat something for me," blurted Ms. Ruby. I opened my eyes and walked to the table, looking past the food and into the kids meal bag. Inside, I found a purple troll toy they were promoting. The troll had glow-in-the-dark yellowish skin, with a purple jacket and neon yellow hair standing straight up. I ate a few fries and instantly felt full. Shay reached her arms out for me to show her the troll toy. She wanted to see it a little closer. I made a few walking gestures across the table with it, until she laughed. She laughed at the toy for several minutes, and then she looked past it, right at me, right into my eyes. It was like she knew that something was wrong with me. That was the first time she'd ever looked at me that way. I wiped my eyes, and forced a smile on my face just for her. She laid her head on the side of the high chair, and stared at me until Ms. Ruby started to speak.

"Devin, baby, remember, this is all just temporary." I knew what she was going to say before she said it. All grown ups were the same. They think they know what to

say to kids to cut off or change feelings. But I just couldn't.

Chapter 15

We pulled up just before sunset. Their house stood by itself in a very clean neighborhood, just off of the main highway in the area. The lawn was very neat and there was a driveway, a garage, and even rocking chairs on the porch. I noticed a young boy on the sidewalk as we began to walk up, and I saw the figure of a very large woman sitting in one of the chairs. Ms. Ruby spoke to them as we walked up, and apologized for taking so long to get there.

"Ain't no problem, Ms. Ruby! How you feelin', suga?" said the large woman. She struggled to stand straight up, due to her weight, and she smiled hard. The woman had on a long, dark dress with flowers all on it, like a church dress.

"And who is THIS??" She said, pointing at Shay, who was hiding her face in Ms. Ruby's shoulder.

"This here is Sha-Lay," said Ms. Ruby, slow enough for the woman to remember.

"Well, hey there, cutie!! I feel like I luh you already!" The woman exclaimed. "And who is this handsome young man here?" She staggered.

"This here is Devin. This one here is my little man!" said Ms. Ruby smiling.

"Hey." I whispered to the woman. She reached out to me for a hug. So, I hugged her, and she held me tight for a few seconds.

"We been waiting on y'all all day. Co- come on, and meet your brother. His name Shawn." The woman said. She grabbed my hand and pulled me behind her to walk towards the boy standing next to the garage. I didn't realize how big the woman was, until I was behind her completely, watching her hips rise and fall with every hard step she took on the sidewalk. She smelled different, like the moisturizer people used for gheri curls. And sweat. We approached the young boy, who looked to be about a year older than me, who wore jeans, a white collar shirt, and a new haircut. Shawn was a couple of inches taller than me and had soft smirk on his face.

"What's up, man??" He said.

"Nothin' much, man." I said smiling while shaking his hand. Ms. Ruby asked the woman if she could come inside and start getting our belongings settled while we kids played. As we walked toward the house, Shawn took my bags out of my hand and asked if he could help get us unloaded. I saw a short, dark skinned man standing in the glass door as we approached. He had a soft voice, and gray stubble where his mustache was supposed to be.

"Well, hello, Ms. Ruby! Hello y'all!" beamed the man. He had a white smile, and a bald head. But I knew that he was a nice person, right then. He had a great positive energy about him and he gave off good vibes. The man helped Shawn and me bring all of our belongings into the house while Shay crawled all over the living room floor. Ms. Ruby and the large woman sat in front of the coffee table, talking and signing different documents.

Shawn walked to the first room in the long hallway, right across from the bathroom, and announced that this was "our room". We had wooden bunkbeds and a matching dresser in the room with a large closet in the corner.

"You on the top bunk," he said, climbing halfway up the bed's ladder. I looked all around, and noticed deodorant, toothpaste and a small cologne bottle sitting on the wooden dresser. The room was spotless. The carpets throughout the entire home were spotless, and the walls seemed extra white as if they were given a fresh coat of paint. Shay's room was just after ours, at the end of the hallway. Her room had a large, white canopy bed in the center, with a storage trunk at the foot of the bed. Matching dresser also accompanied. Her bed linens laid neatly folded at the edge of the dresser, and the room smelled of baby powder. Fresh and new. The parents' room sat across from Shay's room, the largest of them all, with yellow paint, and white bedroom furniture. Both bathrooms were immaculate, with new towels and extra toilet paper neatly tucked away. The mirrors were all clean, and the kitchen looked newly remodeled. After the quick tour, I grabbed Shay to show her to her new room. She looked at me, before I motioned to her that it was okay to roam freely in the room. Although sad, I felt happy for her. She deserved to live in a nice place.

"Alright, so y'all ok?" said a tired Ms. Ruby.

"Yes'm" Shawn and I said together. I was carrying Shay around on my hip, like how Mommy did in the kitchen in the mornings. I realized that she was about to leave, and that this is where we were going to be living going forward. The entire day was exhausting, but for some reason, I felt content. I stared at the large woman waving at Ms. Ruby as she started up the car. That same car had taken us so far that day. I walked up to Ms. Ruby's open window, as she put the car into gear, still holding Shay in my arms. She mouthed the word "temp-o-rary" to me. I nodded my head yes, as I felt a hand on my shoulder. It was the large woman, squeezing me tightly, taking Shay off my shoulder and taking her onto her own. She waved, as Ms. Ruby pulled off, with the same big grin she had when we pulled up. And that was it. We stood on the edge of the sidewalk; me, Shay and this stranger. She kneeled down very carefully, as not to wake Shay who was now snoring on her shoulder, got on one knee, and spoke softly.

"Devin, I know you had a long day, baby, let's get you inside, so that you and Shawn can get a bath before bed."

"No baths, please. Can I take a shower?" I asked. We walked toward the house, and she said that would be fine. I watched the large woman lock the door, while humming softly, what sounded like a gospel tune. Shawn was sitting in the living room watching TV, nodding off to sleep by himself on the couch. I followed her to Shay's room, and helped her to take Shay's shoes off to put her in the big bed by herself.

"Can I sleep in here with her, just for tonight, ma'am? I just don't want her to wake up and not see me anywhere." I asked softly.

"Okay, just for tonight, but you know she's gonna be fine." She asked. "Y'all are gonna be fine." I looked at the floor and nodded yes. She grabbed my face, right in the middle of my chin.

"This is your home now," she whispered.

"Yes, ma'am" I retorted. I walked to the bathroom and took a shower. Shawn sat next to the door, talking to me about everything, and everybody he told all about Shay and me coming today. The woman tucked Shawn in the bed, told us to get some sleep, and turned off the ceiling light in our bedroom. I walked into Shay's bedroom, and overheard Shawn asking her could he come in the room with us, too. He came in shortly after, pillow in hand and an extra blanket to lay on the floor next to the bed. I put the picture frame in the bed between Shay and me, and listened to Shawn continue telling me stories of how he had gotten there, and how he had been there for two years.

"Y'all gonna love it here. I'm gon' let you meet everybody tomorrow." He whispered. "Ms. Tammy gon' show y'all off to everybody, watch."

"Wait, who is that? Who is Ms. Tammy?" I whispered into the darkness. He chuckled at my ignorance.

"That's her name! Our foster mother, bruh!" He laughed as he rolled over. I stared at the ceiling until my eyes got too heavy to keep open. I gripped the picture frame, and fell asleep. I tossed and turned, and even cried a little, in between dreams. This was our new place. I missed Mike, and Ms. Geraldine, and Jeremy, and Mimi. I even missed Ms. Betty.

***

"Da-bieee. Dabieeee!" I opened my eyes to find Shay calling me from the bottom of the bed.

"Hey, Shay, I'm right here." I said. Shay didn't even know that I was right there the entire time. She turned and smiled at me, climbing up on my legs as I stretched. Sometimes, in the mornings, Mommy would have company over and she would always tell me to go outside and play. It was these early mornings that I learned to tell the approximate time by the position of the sun. The sun's position from the window indicated that it was about nine, or ten o'clock in the morning. As I continued to stretch and wake myself up, I smelled fresh grass being cut, and something else. Pancakes! It was pancakes and bacon cooking in the kitchen! Shawn was still asleep next to the bed, drooling on his pillow. I woke him up, hoping that he would walk out of the room first, so that he could show us the way things would work around here. I carried Shay on my back as I followed Shawn into our room.

"That breakfast smells so good!" I exclaimed in a happy voice.

"I know, it would smell extra good, if it was for us." Shawn said, mid yawn.

"What you mean??" I asked.

"We can only eat cereal for breakfast. Da real food is for her and Mr. Buxley." Said Shawn. I figured that he was simply confused with what he said, but nonetheless, we followed him into the kitchen.

"Well, hey, look who's up!" Said Ms. Tammy, leaning over the stove, wearing a very large nightgown. We sat down at the table, I put Shay into my lap, and fixed my eyes on the salt and pepper shakers she was fiddling with.

"Good morning!" Said a smiling Shawn.

"I know y'all had a long day yesterday, so I ain't want to wake y'all up none. But Devin, Shawn gon' tell ya, that we like being up and moving around by seven thirty on my weekends," said Ms. Tammy.

"Yes ma'am" I replied quickly. Something was different about her though, and I couldn't figure it out. It was like all the fake smiles and welcoming friendliness was wearing off. She seemed irritable that maybe we interrupted her normal routine by sleeping late. Mr. Buxley came in the house, talking to himself, and spoke to us all as soon as he saw us.

"Hey kids, how was your sleep?" Mr. Buxley said.

"Good." We both said in unison. He walked to Ms. Tammy, kissed her on the cheek, and grabbed his plate off the stove. He smiled again at us, then went into the living room to watch TV. Ms. Tammy came over to the table and sat two bowls of Captain Crunch in front of Shawn and me. It appeared to be soggy, and I hated soggy cereal.

That whole day, Shawn and I walked around the neighborhood as he showed me everything. Ms. Tammy had members of her church over for lunch, to tell them all about the new kids she had. Shawn introduced me to several neighbors, which included three sisters from a couple houses down from us. The youngest two were the same ages as Shawn and me. He told me where we were to stand for the school bus, and what yards we should never go near. Shawn seemed excited to have me there; I could tell by how much he talked. He managed to even make me laugh a little sometimes. For most of the afternoon, we walked around kicking rocks, while he told me stories of his crush at school. I tried my hardest to listen to him, but I mostly thought of Mommy. I wondered how she was doing. I wondered what Mike was doing, and if the puppies were being fed. I just missed them all. We arrived back at the house around five o'clock, just as the church members were leaving.

"Well, hello!" Said an older woman. "I'm one of your Momma's elders up at your new church. Y'all are gonna love it here. We been praying for all you kids." She said. "I'm gonna see you next Sunday, since y'all missed service today!"

"Yes ma'am" I replied, looking around. Shay was standing at the glass door whining, because she had been left alone. I jogged to the door, and picked her up, tears were in her eyes.

"Dab-bie" She whimpered.

"I know, I was outside with Shawn" I told her. She put her head on my shoulder as we sat down on the couch. Shay reminded me of how lonely I felt all over again. Being outside with Shawn was just like hanging out with a new friend. Being so absorbed in all the new information took my mind off of things for a while. Coming back to see Shay brought me back to the realities that we were in foster care.

"The Simpsons" was coming on just as I began to sink into the left side of the couch. Shay clung to my shoulder while I reached for the remote to turn the volume up.

"What's this?" said Ms. Tammy. I didn't even realize that she'd come in the house so fast. She loomed over Shay and me like a shadow with a different tone in her voice from earlier. She had become bossy and irritable. She went from trying to give us a feeling of family to making me feel like we should be lucky that somebody took us in. It went from 'welcome home' to 'this is my house and you better not forget it'. She made me feel like we owed her something.

"It's The Simpsons." I said in a low voice.

"Uh-hmm, we don't watch no Simpsons in this house, baby; this here a house of the Lord." she shouted. She snatched the remote from me, and changed the channel to The Home Shopping Channel. I sat there for a few minutes in silence, and then took Shay into her room. I grabbed the picture frame off her bed and pointed out each

of us in the picture to Shay.

"Dabbie!" she shouted when I pointed to myself in

the picture.

"Yup!" I said grinning. She clapped her hands and

laughed out loud.

"Shay Shay!!" she shouted when I pointed to her

small face in the picture.

"Yup! You're getting good!" I said.

"Momma!" she shouted when I pointed to Mommy's

face in the picture.

"Yup, Shay you guessed it right." I said, moving my

face away. I felt overcome with tears watching her stare at

Mommy's face in the frame. Reality was beginning to

beam on me like the sun on a hot day. No more days to

count down with Ms. Ruby. No more Baltimore. This was

our new home. A place where nobody knew us.

Shawn's Interlude

I told them to just be happy. Shoot, they was lucky! At least they ended up here in a clean house with Mr. & Mrs. Buxley, and not bounced around from no group homes like me. Last night, I heard him crying in that bed. He ain't know I was still woke, but I was. I kinda feel for him and that little girl, but at least they still together. I keep on telling him, "You in the system now," and when you in the system down here, these people tell you where to go. We ain't got no choice. Hell, I ain't seen my sisters and brothers in three years, since I was 'bout seven. We got took from my momma, and she ain't even tried to find us either. I miss my sisters and brothers everyday, but I can't cry for them no more. Ain't no tears finna help nobody out. That boy just be staring off into space while Ms. Tammy talking to him. He don't know no better. I been here for almost two years from the group home. And I told my case worker not to ever let me leave too. These people good to me; been damn good to me. So, I been being good in school, focused on my studies and all. Mr. Buxley even got me a Gameboy for my good marks in the first quarter. Devin gotta be strong round here, ain't no space for no crying. I know how he feeling, but he gotta get it together. He gon' make me weak, again, crying like that. Ms. Tammy say to pray for them kids, and that's what I been doing. He keeps talking bout how his momma gonna get clean and come for them. Ha! I done heard that a hundred times from them kids in the group home. Something special 'bout him though. He gonna be alright, I know it. Done been round his type before. You gonna pray for them too? Pastor say it's power in numbers. I don't know what that mean, but I just hope y'all will. These group homes and foster homes ain't what they show y'all on TV. All us deserve our own parents. But all parents don't deserve us.

That's what my case worker say. You gonna pray? Pray we

get outta here and pray for them too."- Shawn B

Chapter 16

"How many candles do you see, Shay?" I asked.

"One, T-TWO!!" Shay shouted.

"Make a wish, and blow 'em out!" said Mr. Buxley.

"Pffffffff-whaaaa!" She attempted to blow out all the candles. With help from me and Shawn, she finally blew them all out.

"Yaayyy!!" She screamed. I held back tears while clapping for her second birthday. She looked so pretty. Ms. Tammy had put a white puffy dress on her, with purple and pink ribbons all over. She wore the same colored ribbons in her hair. She and Ms. Tammy laughed together as she turned the kitchen lights back on.

"Who wants cake??" asked Mr. Buxley.

"Me, ME, ME!" Shawn said all three times. He was wearing two birthday hats on his head walking fast behind

Mr. Buxley to the counter, where he was preparing plates of cake and ice cream. It had been two weeks since we'd arrived. And it had taken one day at a time to adjust.

"Does the birthday girl get a special dinner?" I asked Ms. Tammy, who simply laughed at me from the living room.

"Well, there's your answer." Shawn said with a sly grin on his face. We both knew what that meant; canned spaghetti again tonight.

In those days, people that received government assistance had to eat food selected for government programs and they were always generic. Already prepared foods were canned, and given to families on welfare or food stamps. It came in a huge can, with a white label and big black letters, on the side of the can that said "SPAGHETTI". And it tasted like metal, and worms. She'd open one can a week, and that's what we ate for dinner each and every night. I was starting to get tired of the same slop, these new rules, and this fat lady telling me what to do. I kissed Shay goodnight, and wished her a Happy Birthday before going to my own room that night.

"It's not that bad, bro," whispered Shawn.

"Yes, it is. I hate it here." I whispered back.

"Well, you know it's gonna get a little easier everyday. I keep telling you that."

"I know bro, let's just go to sleep, that bus come at six o'clock" I said.

"Yeah it do. Goodnight, Bruh." Shawn answered, yawning.

"Goodnight." I whispered softly. But I didn't feel like it was a good night at all. My chest got tight every time I thought of how happy Shay was at the table. I didn't know whether to smile because she didn't know any better, or to cry, because I did.

The mornings were all the same. Shawn and I got dressed in the dark. We didn't want to turn on the light and tried not to make any noise, as we didn't want to wake Mr. Buxley or Shay. We often put on each other's clothes by mistake by being in the dark. Ms. Tammy would have two soggy bowls of cereal sitting on the table in the kitchen. "He-Man" reruns played on the smallest television I'd ever seen by the table. No matter how much I tried to pay attention, it seemed like the same episode was always on. We'd finish our cereal, put on our jackets for the morning chill, walk out onto the wooden porch in the back and proceed to the bus stop. We only had one bus stop for our entire community. Everybody was ALWAYS quiet in the morning. It was just too early. The poor kids, the rich kids, the farmers' kids, the white kids, the black kids, and then you had us, the "who knows kids". We were all out there, all together, huddled in a silent semi circle, moving around to stay warm. The bus pulled up five minutes late, and stank with diesel fuel, making the forty-five minute ride to school unbearable. Between the kerosene-like smell, and those soggy "Captain Klump-O's," I felt like blowing chunks almost every morning. We'd arrive at Nix Elementary School so early that sometimes, we'd beat the sun up. We'd get off, and begin to thaw out into the hallways. All teachers were white, all classrooms were large, and education was much better than in Baltimore. The fourth grade was spent in one classroom, and one teacher taught us all subjects; Science, Social Studies, Health, Math, and my favorite, Language Arts. Ms. Kay was my teacher. She was a young teacher, three years out of college and dedicated to her young students. Ms. Kay always had a smile, and a certain healthy spunk about her. She always smiled at us, and would ask us how we felt. She was great.

***

"How much candy do you usually get around here?" I asked Shawn. He laughed, sitting close to the mirror on the wall of our room, trying to count underarm hair.

"We don't celebrate it in this here house," said Shawn without even looking up at me.

"No Halloween? That's crazy man, like not at all? No trick or treatin'?" I asked confused.

"Nope. Not at all. And she ain't gonna hear nothin' you tryna say 'bout it either," interrupted Shawn.

My classmates loaded into class on Halloween Day with costumes, face paint, and fake blood. Ms. Kay played Michael Jackson's "Thriller" on a small boombox, and even passed out candy. I was one of two children in the class who hadn't participated in the holiday at all that year. The other student was a Mormon, I believe. Nonetheless, we had fun coloring pages of pumpkins, eating candy, and speaking freely with Ms. Kay.

"I just want to give kudos to a student!" She shouted. "I found one of his writings, that was done on the back of our last pop quiz, by mistake. Devin Dixon." I looked up with a blank stare, completely blushing and taken by surprise, I nodded my head.

"May I share with the class, what you wrote last Tuesday?" She asked.

"Yes ma'am" I said. I racked my brain endlessly trying to remember what I'd written, before she cleared her throat…

"Unseen, Unheard"

If Mimi was here, she'd tell me to pick my head up, and to get myself focused.
But she isn't.
I've stared hard enough at the walls in this room, that I have become them.
I finished this quiz so fast, that I have become the walls.
Hard and cold.
Like Ma must be.

I hate you so much. I hate you so much. I hate you so

much.

You made me like these walls.

Unseen by these strangers around me!!

I saw a dandelion in the bathroom- a few minutes ago.

And it made me think of you.

Bright enough to know its color,

Drowned in bubbles all shades of misty blue.

-For Dorray (If I remember you)

10/21/93

"Wow, Devin." said Ms. Kay.

I buried my face into my hands as I could feel the kids turning around to look at me. The bell seemed to ring with perfect timing that afternoon. Desks moved, and students filed out of the classroom before I could even respond. I packed my backpack and ran for the classroom door. I felt a hard jerk on my back as I crossed the doorway. It was Ms. Kay grabbing me.

"Can I have a hug young man? I wasn't trying to embarrass you." She hugged me tight with a bright smile. "You're gonna be something special someday kiddo," she said with water forming in her eyes.

***

I watched the candy shake as the floorboards creaked when she walked over them. A vampire and a dead bride came to our door when "The Simpsons" went to a commercial break. We were allowed to watch it because it was Halloween. I blew out hot air, watching her greet the kids that came to the door, handing them candy. I didn't understand how if we couldn't celebrate because we lived in a house of the Lord, how could she celebrate with the neighborhood kids? She was a performer, an actress that knew just when to turn it on. I was growing to be disgusted of her. And I think she knew it.

Chapter 17

By the time Christmas rolled around, I was emotionally numb. Sundays were an all-day church rally, Saturdays were basically a sleep day. The week blended days and nights together, ending with Mrs. Buxley eating caramel corn on the worn couch, watching "Supermarket Sweep". She was upset with me since report cards came out. I wasn't allowed to leave the house or play with anything at all, because of the "B" I brought home in math class. I explained to her that I had missed the section in math about fractions, due to changing schools so many times. But she didn't care about whatever I had to say about school.

By Christmas Eve, the school was buzzing with excitement about Christmas. By now, I had warmed up a little to the other students. We sat in class that day, coloring pictures for the troops overseas. We were in school, but hadn't been learning anything all week, mostly playing

games, finishing extra credit assignments and helping Ms.

Kay clean up our classroom. That night, Shawn and I

stayed up late, taking turns reading The Berenstein Bears

books to Shay. We were all excited about Christmas, but I

missed Mommy more than usual.

"Sometimes, you don't ever wonder?" I whispered.

"What are you talkin' now?" huffed Shawn.

"Wonder what they doing? What Christmas would

be like if you still lived with your family?" I asked.

"See, what you gotta do is, just let it go," he

explained. I knew that he could tell by the look on my face,

that I hadn't understood.

"See, you ain't gonna make it like this man! She

ain't gonna understand how to make it here, unless you just

leave the past alone. Our mommas out there doin' who

knows what, and they come back if they feel like it. End of

story. But whiles I'm here, and you here, and SHE here, we

got to shut up and be thankful. Be thankful, Devin," he scolded.

Shay was nodding off on the makeshift pallet we made on our bedroom floor. We looked through old comic books until we both drifted away to sleep ourselves.

Chapter 18

I woke up with one eye barely open on Christmas

morning! Shay was tossing all around in between Shawn

and me, and Shawn hadn't moved a muscle for the entire

night. I nudged him until he woke too. Shay clapped her

hands, and waved her arms up and down singing a song

from church while we ran to the living room. It was

beautiful! The big Douglass Fir had taken up the entire

corner of the living room. And the gifts! The GIFTS!! The

gifts overflowed out onto the floor itself. It was amazing, it

must've been one hundred boxes! All sizes, large and

small, and in the most beautiful wrapping paper I'd ever

seen. We watched the boxes shake when we heard Ms.

Tammy coming through the long hallway toward us all.

"Don't touch nothin' at all y'all!" She shouted. She

was out of breath by the time her toes reached the living

room's area rug. We all sat in front of the tree, while Mr. Buxley fumbled around with an old camera. He smiled, and made us smile.

"CHEESE!!" Shawn and I shouted. Shay was getting restless in my lap, so Ms. Tammy told me to let her go.

"All them ones in the Sesame Street wrapping paper is hers," she said. I passed Shay a small box with Bert and Ernie on it and we all laughed at the sounds she made looking at the paper. Shawn reached for the biggest one, a HUGE box in a shiny blue tin-like paper. Shawn started ripping paper off the package, while Mr. Buxley looked at me with a grin and whispered, "Dig in." We tore through boxes for almost a half hour!! There was so much stuff there! I finally got the handheld games that I wanted! But I nearly passed out when I opened the final one with my name on it. I knew what it was as soon as I saw the iconic blue color at the top of the package. It was 'Paperboy'! The game that I've been wanting for the entire year! I jumped up, falling all over the toys Shay had scattered on the floor and hugged Mr. Buxley. Shawn and Shay laughed hard at how happy I was. I even ran up to Ms. Tammy and hugged her.

"Now, before you get too happy, you need to understand something, Devin," she said. I backed out of our embrace, and looked at her with a puzzled look, I was confused. She looked upset all of a sudden. Mr. Buxley started picking up the paper off the living room floor while I sat on my knees still gazing at Ms. Tammy.

"Now I told you, that if you didn't get that B up to a A, that you wasn't gon' have no Christmas. And I meant what I said, boy".

I huffed at what she was implying.

"But, Ms. Tammy, you know I been tryin' real hard with my math. I, I told yo.."

"I don't wanna hear it" she interrupted. "So, what you gonna do is go through all that stuff and pick out one." She said, rolling her eyes.

"One gift?" I asked. "You mean, I only get to keep one?"

"Ye-UP," she shouted. "And you lucky I'm lettin' you keep one, cus I wasn't gon' let you keep nothin!" She walked through the living room and into the kitchen like she just didn't ruin my Christmas.

Her words rang in my ear like a steel drum as she came back into the room and went towards Shay. I sat on my knees and stared at her directly in her eyes, while she avoided looking into mine. She was playing with Shelae's new "Jack in the Box" toy. Shawn motioned for me from the corner to help him move the big box toward the garage and even though I saw him, I couldn't move. I felt lethargic. I couldn't believe her. One gift? One gift, yo? What was the point of even having me open all of that stuff? She couldn't even look at me. Like she knew she was wrong. Shawn cleared his throat, and motioned for me to come to the kitchen with him. I finally got up, and let the Paperboy game fall onto the floor where I was sitting. I looked back at her when I reached the kitchen.

"Look, I know you mad, but calm down." Shawn whispered.

"Calm DOWN? Calm Down! That fat ass just took all my toys from me man!! What the hec-?"

"Shut yo mouth!!" he interrupted. "That lady don't owe ya nothin'!"

I leaned against the refrigerator with both hands balled into fists. I wanted to cry but I couldn't. My ears rang with anger. Anger because it just didn't feel like it was right, and the tears because what Shawn said was true. After sulking in the kitchen for a few more minutes, I nudged past Ms. Tammy in the living room, picked up all remaining wrapping paper, and slipped into my room as she loudly talked on the phone. She smacked candy corn loudly into the receiver, bragging to the church sisters on the line. She bragged about all the toys she bought for us but never saying how she only let me keep one. As I picked up the remnants of what should have been a great Christmas, she never even looked at me. She never even acknowledged my presence in the room. I felt unimportant and invisible.

I felt even more unimportant when she made me go with her to return all of the toys that she got me. Except Paperboy.

I lay down on my back on the carpet in the bedroom, thinking a lot, but not allowing my tears to fall. I heard Shay laughing up and down the hallway, as Mr. Buxley faked chased her with her new toy vacuum cleaner. I stared at the ceiling, wondering what Christmas was like in Baltimore. I wondered if it had snowed, and if my whole family was still the same as the last time I'd seen them. I wondered if Mimi still left my coat by the front door. But I mostly imagined Mommy showing up to get us, that very day. I wondered how she was, and if she had been thinking of us. I missed real food, and being around real family. I felt so loud, but quiet at the same time. Like I could feel how much my heart was breaking, but if I screamed as loud as I could, the only people who would've cared, would merely hear a soft mumble from the south. Mumbles that had too often went unheard along with subtle cries, and unfamiliar scenery, through lenses unpreferred.

Valentine's Day came and went. It was a blustery winter in the south that year. Over the months since Christmas, I'd allowed myself to go numb. School was the same each day. I think I had lost my ability to be fake about what I was feeling inside. Ms. Tammy began to make me write book reports each evening after school, just before dinner. She said it was until I 'straightened myself out'. I knew that she meant the new attitude that I was carrying around. I stopped trying to be phony and pretend that everything was ok. I began to show that everything was not ok. I would answer her questions before she finished asking them. My responses to her were quick and short. I became irritable and didn't want to be bothered. I stopped trying to be nice. It wasn't just Christmas that changed me. It was the way Ms. Tammy would treat me once the front door closed. She wasn't abusive or anything but she was a great actress. She would put on her wig and we would go to church and she just acted like the perfect foster mother. At home, she barely spoke to me. If I was excited about something, she would find a way to get on me and kill my joy. The whole situation just changed me. Not being with Mommy and trying to just survive. In February, I started spending some time in the garage, mostly right before the sun set for the night. I was never in there longer than 30 minutes, but it always felt just long enough for me. In the garage, I found old tools, books, and some other stuff I never knew existed. This is where Mr. Buxley's belongings seemed to have all ended up. I even started reading some of the books that I found there. I would crack the garage door, just enough to feel the winter's cold on my toes as I read different fables from the school's library. The best part about the garage is that I was often out of sight, so I was also out-of-mind. Ms. Tammy couldn't fit down the narrow doorway to pester me there so it was cool. Like a cave in many ways to a young man.

Shawn and Shay got a lot closer over the winter and he was really becoming a big brother to us both. We'd sometimes race to the car on Sundays after church, we'd pass notes in Sunday school, and practice dance moves in the garage together. Shawn was my only friend. When the spring started coming in, we shared a root beer in the garage doorway watching the sun set.

"Hey, what do you see when you be staring out there, into the clouds like that?" asked Shawn.

"What? What you mean?" I asked, confused. I broke my stance against the door and turned to him.

"I be talking to you sometimes, and you don't even hear me." he said, laughing.

"I dunno. Guess just seeing stuff. Thinking, you know?" I said.

"Well, can you STOP thinking so much!!" He laughed. He reached for my arm, and we laughed as I helped him to a standing position. We stared into the woods just as the sun said goodnight to us both.

"You know Ms. Ruby been calling for you, right?" Shawn said in a low tone.

"Been calling here? At this house?" I asked.

"Yup, and Ms. Tammy wasn't finna tell you. At least not yet." He scoffed, "You should see what she been calling for, bruh." He added. My head spun with amazement, as I closed the garage door. Shawn told me to go ahead and that he would lock up in the garage, and motioned for me to go speak with Ms. Tammy. I walked up the steps, and found her on the couch attempting to paint her nails. Her double chin held the house phone to her ear.

"Hey, oh, I didn't know you was on the phone." I said, backing away.

"Well, what you want? You done came up here now." She said.

"H-has, Ms. Ru-Ms. Ms. Ruby been calling?" I asked.

Her eyes got wide. "Sister Regina, I'm gon' call you tomorrow." She said just before hanging up. She sat up in the worn chair, after a long stretch, and began to chuckle. "Yeah, she did! She said she was speaking to your momma, something about her time in the rehab. You can call Ms. Ruby whenever you want to, I'm not gon' stop that." She looked up at me from the melting ice cream in her favorite bowl, and smiled.

"Thank you." I whispered. I padded softly to my room, and heard Shawn mumbling the words to a rap song from the closet. I smiled as I climbed the ladder to my bed. I felt good, like the Universe had finally answered my cries.

***

"Good morning, Sweetie!" said Ms. Ruby.

"Good morning!" I shouted back into the phone. It was an early spring morning when I finally heard her voice.

"I been trying to reach you, to let you know that I spoke to your Momma. She's doing so well in rehab, and she wants to see you and your sister, Devin!"

I nearly dropped the phone when Ms. Ruby said that, out of excitement.

"Really?? You spoke to her?!" I asked, excited.

"Yes, and as a matter of fact, hang up, stay by the phone. I'm gon' call you right back," she said.

When the line went blank, I hung the phone up on the receiver. Smiling at the wall, I couldn't believe it! She actually spoke to Mommy! Mommy asked about Shay and me. I ran down the hallway, only to discover that Shay wasn't in her bed. She must've left with Mr. And Ms. Buxley to go to the local flea market. Shawn's voice bellowed from the bathroom as I breezed by and he was singing his own horrible rendition of Sade's "Smooth Operator" in the shower. The phone began to ring as I touched the floor of the kitchen. I snatched the phone off the hook without thinking.

"Good morning, Buxley's residence." I said.

"Hey, Devin! Devin are you there?" Ms. Ruby asked.

"Yes ma'am, Yes, I'm here. Can you hear me?" I asked.

"Hey, yeah Devin, I'm here. Hang on a sec," she said. The line went blank for almost three seconds. I heard echoes and several voices in the background.

"Hello, Hello??" said a voice.

"Hey, yes, hello??" I answered.

"Hey, Dev, how you doin, baby!!??" she said. I paused. I completely froze. I paused. Like completely forgot what day it was, what time it was. And my chest tightened.

It was her.

"Ma. M..-Ma, Mo-mmy?" I sniffled.

"Yeah, honey, hey!!" said Mommy. My ears went deaf, my mind went dumb, my head went blank. I was in so much disbelief from actually hearing her voice, the phone fell right out of my hands. By the time I picked the phone back up, she was crying on the line, and so was Ms. Ruby.

"Hey, Ma!" I answered.

"Hey, Dev!! How are you!? How is Shay?!" she asked. I told her that we were both good, and that we were safe, and together. We all cried on the phone together for at least twenty minutes. But it felt like a lifetime. Mommy's voice was strong, and broken at the same time. I could hear that she was sober and clear headed, yet I could hear and feel the emotions in her words. I could hear her smile through the phone! She told me that she was done with rehab, and that she was coming for us. She said that she is due for a visit, and that Ms. Ruby was gonna set it up! I had never been happier in MY LIFE!

Chapter 19

"Well, this is the place, sports fans!" said Ms. Ruby wiping a nervous sweat from her brow. One week had passed by since I spoke to my mother on the phone, and it was a Friday afternoon when we pulled up at the rehab facility where Mommy was staying. I was still in shock, during the hour-long drive, that Ms. Tammy even let me leave school early. I woke Shelae up in her car seat, making sure she'd be alert by the time we saw Mommy. Ms. Ruby carried her heavy leather briefcase, and I carried Shay to the front desk. It was beginning to get warm outside. Nothing went as imagined. I thought about this day for the last six months, every day. I thought they'd have Mommy in a jail-like building, with guards, and shackled prisoners walking about. But instead, we were greeted by smiling, cheerful, recovering addicts. They were so nice to us, the receptionist even gave Shay and me a lollipop. Ms. Ruby led us down a very long hallway, lined with pictures, poems, and certificates of completion. Truly a beautiful building. We walked out of an open door that led to a wide spread clearing, almost like a field. There were families at over a dozen wooden picnic tables, talking, laughing and crying. Shay gripped me tight as we walked through the field. She wasn't comfortable around this many strangers, and the long ride left her kind of irritable. Ms. Ruby mumbled several things to me, that I couldn't make out over the chatter from the tables. We walked until the grass seemed extra green. And then I heard it.

"There's my babies!"

My ears went numb, my neck felt hot, and my vision sharpened. There stood Mommy, arms gaped open, with the brightest smile, she'd ever worn. She wore a dress with pink flowers all over it! She ran to me, because I couldn't feel my legs under me anymore!

Her warm tears ran down the side of my face, as we embraced. She smelled fresh, and clean! She squeezed Shay and me so hard. We cried. We cried. And. We. Cried.

When she backed away, Shay looked her in her eyes, with a confused look on her face for a moment. Like she had forgotten who she was. Mommy took her out my arms.

"Hey baby!! My Shay!! I missed you so much!!" Mommy shrieked.

Shelae gave her a small smirk, then burst into laughter as Mommy hugged her harder. I felt like I was floating. Ms. Ruby stood by the picnic table wiping tears from her bifocals. Some of the other women at the tables applauded our reunion. It was a perfect moment. In those seconds, my fears, my wants, my complaints, anger and depression were all gone. My mommy was here. A familiar face was in front of us again, and she was happy to see us!! We sat at the table and she held my hand the entire time. She asked me how school was, and what was my favorite subjects. I told her all about the Buxleys, and how much I never stopped thinking about her.

"I'm getting things lined up, Devin. I already found us a place and everything!!" Mommy said. I couldn't stop smiling. She was so happy.

"Mommy, you look so good!" I said.

"I know, all chunky and healthy-looking," said Ms. Ruby. Mommy told us that she was sorry for leaving us, and asked me to forgive her for what led us to foster care. I held her hand, looking over her nails, and I didn't even care about any of that anymore. Because Mommy was right here. No pictures, no dreams; she was right there, in front of me. The moment was surreal!!

"Devin, what you know 'bout a place called Columbia?" Mommy asked.

"Nothing." I said shrugging my shoulders.

"Well, that's where we goin' at. That's gonna be where our fresh start is gonna happen!" She said.

I immediately turned to Ms. Ruby, who was playing patty cake with Shay.

"You excited?" Ms. Ruby asked.

"Yes, Ma'am!" I screamed.

Ms. Ruby pointed over to a playground that was on the other side of the picnic tables, and asked me to go and play for a few minutes while she and Mommy discussed some paperwork that she needed her to sign. I kissed Shay on the cheek and ran over to the swings that sat by themselves on a sand mound. The warm sun beamed down on me harder than it ever had before. I felt like the entire day was a fast dream, that you've had many times before. It felt like the day was a blur, everything was happening so fast and it seemed like I was floating. It all was a bit overwhelming. Mommy's smile radiated as she waved to me from the picnic table. I watched other people and their family members gather on the baseball diamond for an impromptu game of kickball. Through all the shouts and cheers, I still heard Ms. Ruby's occasional laugh. I swung on the swings with my head back, almost doing a flip each time I went backwards. I felt free. Free enough to not be in fear. Those minutes went by fast enough for me to appreciate them, but slow enough for me to remember them.

She made me promise that I wouldn't cry as we had to leave her at the front desk. She hugged Shay and whispered something in her ear before letting her go. I'd forgotten how beautiful she was. Her skin glowed a sun-kissed caramel color, her eyes were white, and wide. Her face was clear, and her weight looked good on her. I caught myself gazing at her when she reached for me. Her jean jacket smelled like Jovan Musk, and cotton balls. That was Mommy's signature scent. I buried my eyes deep into her jean jacket. Trying to hold onto the moment forever.

"One more month, Devin. We're gonna be back together by summer," she whispered.

I looked up at her, and saw that her tears matched the ones I was trying desperately to hold back. I squeezed her tight, and told her goodbye. She hugged Ms. Ruby. "Tempo-rary, Dorray," she mouthed to her. Ms. Ruby held my hand and carried Shay to the car.

We pulled off, and I noticed a white lady come out and hugged Mommy in the distance. I sat back in my seat and began day dreaming of the day that we would be back together again.

Chapter 20

The Pastor shook my hand extra hard on a bright Sunday in spring. He stood in his purple robe, and watched us exit with a sweet smile on his face.

"Sister Buxley! You almost forgot your Bible!" he shouted from the church steps. Ms. Tammy waved at him, and motioned for me to go and retrieve it from him.

"Thank you," I said when I grabbed the Bible into my hands, from his.

"Take care of them, son." he said. He smiled at me, and walked back into the church as I nodded my head. The entire ride home, Shawn giggled at the three leaf clover he'd picked for Shay to keep.

"I- I thought it was one of the lucky ones, Mama!! Brr-hahahaha!!" he exclaimed. Shay looked confused at him, while holding the stem.

"Flu-wah" she said.

"Yup, Shay, that's right!! Flow-wer," I said. Her hair was in seven or eight pretty plaits with pink barrettes at the ends.

Ms. Tammy had been rather quiet over the last few weeks since the visit with Mommy. Mr. Buxley hummed the tune to an old western movie as we pulled into a Shoney's parking lot for an early dinner. The one time we came here before, we sat in the same place, right next to the bathroom, where Ms. Tammy felt the most comfortable. She stared at me as she finished her second plate of bacon.

"What you smiling so hard for lil' boy?"

I stopped playing the tic tac toe game on my kids menu and looked at her with a puzzled look.

"Whatchu mean, Mrs. Buxley?" I asked.

"Oh, you know what I mean," she said with bits of bacon flying from her mouth.

"Come on, Honey, leave the boy be now," interrupted Mr. Buxley.

"Nah, it ain't none of that!" she answered. "He been round here walkin' round on his high horse!" She shouted. "I just can't wait for your ungrateful self to get outta my house anyway!"

I looked over at Shawn who was now poking his fried chicken with his fork.

"Ms. Tammy, I am not on no high horse. I'm just happy cuz time coming soon for us to go back to my mother! She clean now, you know? We gotta move back home soon!" I said, slamming my fork onto the plastic tablecloth.

She wiped her mouth with her handkerchief and laughed a deep, billowy laugh as she slumped back into her chair. None of us at the table said anything because we knew what she meant by the remark. She snarled her lip up and scolded me from across the table for the next 45 minutes until we left.

Her silence, like always, shouted so much to me.

She was angry; like really angry at the thought of us actually leaving and I didn't understand why. Why would she be upset that Shay and I were returning back to where we belonged?

The next morning, I looked at myself in the mirror with the damp washcloth in my hand.

"Today is gonna be FUN." I whispered to myself.

It was the day of the Spring Fling at school. My teacher said that we didn't even need to bring our notebooks to school on this final Friday of the month. I had heard so much about the Spring Fling from last year from all the other kids at school. A whole day of fun, with grilled food, summer treats, and games amongst each grade. We would play tug of war, participate in a scavenger hunt, and there would even be a moon bounce! It was gonna be so cool! And the day was finally here! I ran to the bus stop and Shawn walked behind me very slowly.

"What's wrong with you?" I asked.

"It's just not fair!" he shouted. "Elementary kids get to have all the fun!" Shawn continued. He was mad because junior high kids didn't have a Spring Fling and he remembered how much fun he knew I was gonna have today.

I chuckled at his anger while throwing dirt mounds at him from the mailbox. He returned fire though, and was laughing at me within minutes. My "brother" and I giggled in the crisp spring air until the bus pulled up.

When we got to school, I'd been directed to the cafeteria to get my class color.

"ALL FOURTH GRADERS GET BLUE SHIRTS!!" Shouted Mr. Barnwell, our Phys. Ed. teacher.

My classmates and I talked aimlessly and making underarm farts while we stood single-file in line to go to the gymnasium to get our blue shirts. All of our teachers were already in there, ready to get an early game of dodgeball against the third graders, who were wearing green tee shirts, and were obviously getting antsy. It was perfect! We clobbered them! I laughed harder than I ever had that afternoon. We sat and ate popsicles in the courtyard while we waited for tug of war to start. We sang songs while the fifth graders stood around in gray shirts, desperately trying to dunk our Principle in the dunk tank. It was perfect. We sang along to Vanilla Ice's "Ice Ice Baby", while getting our faces painted on the front lawn of the school. Nobody did school work. The teachers were laughing, the students were laughing, and we all ate endless amounts of grilled hot dogs and hamburgers. The entire day left most of us exhausted, and asleep on the school bus on the way home. Shawn shook me awake.

"Look, boy, you droolin! Hahahaha!" Shawn laughed at me as I wiped the gaping wad of spit I had in the corners of my mouth. We ran home from the bus stop, and found Ms. Tammy on the porch speaking to one of her church sisters.

"Good afternoon, ladies" I said with a smile.

Shawn waved at the pair of women as we walked toward the door.

"Hey, Devin?" Shouted Ms. Tammy.

'Yes'm?" I said quickly.

"Ms. Ruby said call her," she retorted as she turned back to her company.

I ran to the phone in the kitchen and dialed Ms. Ruby's desk number. Shawn and I were still laughing when she picked up the phone.

"How does two weeks sound, Devin?" I almost dropped the phone from my clammy hands when I heard her say the words. I knew what that meant.

"S-sounds great to me!" I exclaimed.

"Hey, that's what I figured!!" Ms. Ruby gleamed. "She done found a place, and a job!! Can you believe it? She already done found a job and everything!!" Ms. Ruby sounded so excited! And I was too!

It was really happening. All the prayers, the overthinking, the anxiety, it was coming to an end. In two weeks, Shay and I were going home! Home! Between the day I had in school, and from the conversation I had with Ms. Ruby, I felt as if I was walking on clouds that night. Shawn and I played a couple hands of "I Declare War" in Shay's room on the floor while she drifted away to sleep. We had the windows open, and were drinking canned cream sodas that I'd bought home from the Spring Fling.

Chapter 21

I stood tall, on a warm afternoon in the late spring, staring at my muscles in the mirror. My shirtless chest seamed to be missing some hair, not that I'd ever had any on my chest, but for some reason that day, I felt younger than I was. Shawn popped me with his towel when he entered the room, which made me yelp like a puppy.

"What was that for?" I shouted while rubbing my back.

"Cus you leavin! Gotta hit you now while I can!" laughed Shawn.

I sat next to the window of our room looking around, when I felt my chest tightening. He was looking around too. I think that we both knew that the times we shared in this tiny room were over. He mumbled words under his breath while I kicked at the strap on my suitcase.

"She here!!" shrieked Ms. Tammy, walking by our room like a big, blue, blur.

Shawn grabbed Shay's suitcase in the hallway, and I grabbed mine. As I walked down the hallway of the house that day, the blue carpet seemed cleaner, like it was brand new. Almost like I'd never seen it before. Ms. Tammy had already let Shay out, and she was playing patty cake with Ms. Ruby by the time I got to the door.

"There's my big man!" she shouted. I ran and hugged her with all my might.

"You 'bout ready??" she asked.

"Yes'm," I said quickly.

Ms. Tammy eased off the porch with a small smirk on her face towards Ms. Ruby, but something was different about her. She was walking a bit slower, and she was quiet that whole day. Just a handful of words from her, all day! I walked to the edge of the lawn as Mr. Buxley pulled into the garage. Shawn tossed me the baseball from our bedroom.

"You gonna remember me by it??" he said.

I swiped sweat from my forehead, and nodded yes. We stood in front of each other tossing the ball back and forth when Mr. Buxley interrupted.

"Well, well, Mr. Devin, you and Ms. Shay are out of here huh??"

"Yes, sir!" I replied.

He stretched his arms out and gave me a hug while he carried grocery bags into the house. He whispered in my ear, "It was a pleasure having y'all here. Keep on keepin on! And take care of your sister, hear?"

I stepped back and smiled at him, "Yes, sir." I whispered.

Out of the corner of my eye, I saw Ms. Ruby motioning for me to come along. Ms. Tammy and Shawn were giving Shay goodbye kisses in her car seat. Ms.

Tammy leaned way back when I walked up to her. The horrible wig was cocked to the right side way too far to be taken seriously.

"I wasn't too bad to you, was I?" she asked.

I shook my head no, and gave her a hug. She slowly got down on one knee so we were almost eye level and gave me another hug. But she didn't let go right away. I opened my eyes and looked over her shoulder at Shawn, who looked as confused as I was. She pulled me away, and kissed me on my cheek. She had tears in her eyes. She was crying.

"I'm only hard on you, 'cus I know how strong you gon' have to be, baby. Ms. Tammy love you, hear?" she cried. She got up and walked away from me abruptly.

The screen door slammed as Shawn walked up to me with a high five. Ms. Ruby started the car, and changed the radio station.

"Gon' miss you, man." Shawn said with a gasping voice.

"I'm gon' miss you, too, man." I said, reaching for him. We held each other, and let each other go, each of us with tears in our eyes.

"You better be writing them book reports, you hear!" He screamed as I closed the car door.

"Yeah, uh-huh, you know I ain't!" I screamed out of the half open window.

Ms. Ruby laughed and began out of the driveway. Shawn ran to the edge of the lawn and waved into the car at Shay.

"Hey, Devin, don't forget about me man! Write about me in your essays! Send me some letters!" he shouted.

"I will!" I screamed to him.

Ms. Ruby turned onto the main road and pulled away fast. His lanky frame got smaller behind us as I stared out the window at him. I sat back in my seat, smiling at Shay, and closed my eyes while the warm breeze blew over my face. Ms. Ruby sang along to the tune of "Love Come Down" floating down the interstate towards our new life.

Chapter 22

"We are here!!" Shouted Ms. Ruby. She turned the radio down, as I opened my eyes. I saw a huge high school that read SPRING VALLEY HIGH on its plaquard in front of the large campus. It was about about three-thirty in the afternoon when we turned into the bright apartment complex. I woke Shay in her car seat, and she 'oohh-ed' and 'ahh-ed' at the pretty flowers and neatly landscaped grounds. There were kids outside playing and adults outside talking as we drove through. We pulled around the complex in Ms. Ruby's car, and I was shocked at how beautiful the scenery was. The grass was bright and green and there were so many trees. The complex looked new and freshly painted. The structures weren't run down and the grounds were clean. This was unlike any other place we'd lived. This place did not look like Section 8.

Ms. Ruby parked the car, and checked the address with her paperwork that she'd had in her briefcase after she turned the engine off. A butterfly fluttered outside of Shay's window while I stretched my legs in the back seat. Ms. Ruby got out of the car first.

"Come on y'all. Devin, you excited to see ya momma?" she asked.

"Yes, ma'am," I replied reluctantly. We had been through this so much in the past, that I second guessed what was happening. I couldn't believe this day was finally here, yet, I was still questioning her recovery and if she would stay clean.

I took Shay out of her car seat and noticed a slim, short, latino woman emerge from the steps in front of the building where we parked, smoking a cigarette. She looked at us in a very strange way, stroking her cigarette lighter softly. We had never seen her before but she looked at us as if we were familiar to her.

"Hello." Ms. Ruby said to the woman.

"Hola," said the lady. "Wait, oh wait!!" she exclaimed with a heavy spanish accent. "You mus be a Ms. Ru-Bee!" she practically screamed.

Ms. Ruby nodded her head slowly. The woman flicked her cigarette smiling very hard, and ran up the stairs in white flip flops. Ms. Ruby turned to me as if to ask "who was that?" I just shrugged my shoulders and grabbed the bags from the trunk.

And then I heard it.

"My babies!!" shrieked a voice that I knew. A smiling face came running down the steps in an all white dress that clung to her body. It was Mommy! She ran and slammed her body into Ms. Ruby's before any of us could understand what was happening.

"Dorray!!" cried Ms. Ruby into Mommy's shoulder. The two embraced for a long time while Shay and I stood looking on. The slim hispanic woman appeared behind

Mommy, wiping her own tears away, with a smile.

Mommy and Ms. Ruby were whispering something to each other in a tone low enough that I couldn't make out. She let Ms. Ruby go, and grabbed for Shay. She picked Shay up and swung her around. Shay laughed as her feet dangled.

"Aww!" shouted a sobbing Ms. Ruby.

I clapped my hands and released a huge sigh of relief from deep within.

"MY SON!!" Mommy shouted, and grabbed me hard. Mommy held me like she's never done before. Although I promised myself and Shawn that I wouldn't, I still cried. I cried hard into her dress and she cried too. She held me, and for the first time in a long time, I could breathe again. I felt whole again. Complete. Important. She stood back from me, and laughed, looking at me through new eyes.

"You've gotten so tall, Devin!!" she shouted.

"Thanks, Ma!!" I said shyly, glancing at my feet.

"This- this my friend, Maritza, y'all! We were in recovery together, and ended up right across the hall from each other in these beautiful apartments!"

I looked over at Ms. Maritza who was already hugging Ms. Ruby and Shay. She kneeled down, and smiled at me with tears in her eyes. She didn't say anything, just hugged me tight and I returned her hug with the same strength. I could tell that she was as happy as Mommy was to finally see us. It was perfect! The warm summer sun smiled down on us.

All was right in the world!

I carried our bags up to the second landing of the building, and up to Apartment 203, in the back. Ms. Ruby told Mommy that she needed to hurry and get some paperwork signed so she could get back before her office closed. On my last trip with the bags, Mommy pointed across the hall to where Ms. Maritza lived.

Ms. Maritza explained to me, in very broken english, "My son, he and my daughta, they live here too! He same age, you."

I beamed a quick smile to her, and backed into the apartment for a better look at the new house. It was HUGE!! High ceilings, clean carpeted floors, open living room and dining area, a room for me, a room for Shay, two bathrooms, a huge bedroom for Mommy, and a patio with a sliding door! It was amazing!

"Dev, you can see both playgrounds from the patio, baby!" shouted Mommy, as she handed Ms. Ruby back her pen. I ran through the house, and into my room and jumped onto my bed.

"My own room!" I gasped to myself. I opened the closet and imagined how many toys would fit. Shay ran into my room and jumped onto the bottom of the bed laughing. I picked her up and we lay there looking at the ceiling, smiling. I was so excited! It was perfect! Mommy had done it! All on her own!

We closed the front door and walked Ms. Ruby downstairs to her car. She slipped me a card with her numbers on it before hugging Mommy for the last time.

"See, Dorray, temp-por-ary," she whispered to Mommy, who was already crying again.

"Didn't I tell you, Devin, didn't I tell you!!" she shouted. I hugged her again, and thanked her for all that she'd done. "You call me at this number if you need anything! And you take care of Baby Girl, no matter what, you hear me?" she said.

"Yes ma'am, I will!!" I retorted.

"I'm gon' come check in on y'all in a lil' while, but for now, just enjoy! Y'all done been through so much!! Dorray, don't let me down, alright?" she said as she pulled back from the parking spot.

"No, ma'am! Never again! Never!" said Mommy, following the car with her eyes. Shay laid her head down on Mommy's shoulder while Ms. Ruby pulled away with a bright smile, into the southern sunset. I felt her hand on mine as we watched her pull away. "Ready to go home, Dev?" asked Mommy in a low tone.

I looked into her teary eyes, wiped my nose, and mouthed, "yes ma'am," as we walked up the steps into our new home. Together. All of Us. Never to be apart again.

The first few days, we slept in Mommy's bed with her, watching TV, crying at times, as I updated her on our whole experience in foster care. I told her all about the Buxley's and Shawn, and school, and church, and the neighborhood out in the country. At times, we found ourselves in the dining room eating pancakes and popsicles at the table in our nightclothes. Mommy told us endless stories of rehab, the women she'd met, her cleansing process, the stories they told, her meetings and about how much she'd missed us. She had taken three days off from work, just so she could be home with us for the first few days. It was awesome! Sometimes, I would wake to Mommy on the side of her bed praying, crying and thanking God for having us back with her. Sometimes, I would wake up, and look all around to make sure this wasn't all a dream. I noticed that I slept deeper here then at the Buxley's. I dreamt about Shawn, and often wondered how he was doing.

Mommy, Shay, and I caught the bus down into town to go to Blockbuster Video to pick up some movies, and so Mommy could show us around Columbia. Mommy walked us down into the biggest Walmart I'd ever seen, right off of Two Notch Road. It was a beautiful, abundant, clean little town with hard working residents.

"Perfect place to build." Mommy said.

I was excited to get back home, and burst open the microwave popcorn, and snacks we'd picked up from

Blockbuster. I dropped the bag waiting for Mommy to open the door. Shay ran around the entire floor of the hallway laughing and giggling to herself when I heard a voice from behind me.

"Hey, wha-wha- what'd you get?" said the voice.

I turned around and noticed a short kid with thick, dark, curly hair standing in front of Ms. Maritza's door. He smiled as I stared at him.

"Oh, hey." I said, smiling.

"I'm Alvin!" he said abruptly.

"Yeah, Dev, that's Ms. Maritza's son," shouted Mommy from our apartment.

"Oh, what's up, man!" I said to him. "A Bronx Tale, and Blank Check." I said, as we shook hands.

"Oh! I never he-hu-heard of dem," he said stammering heavily. He waved and went into his own house before I could say anything else.

I watched "A Bronx Tale" first, eating fistfuls of the popcorn from Mommy's big metal bowl. I cried a little to myself as the credits rolled at the end. Mommy and Shay snored behind me on her bed. I fell asleep myself in front of the bed waiting for the tape to rewind to the beginning.

Chapter 23

After about a week, Alvin started asking me to come over, so that he'd have someone to play his Sega Genesis with. We would play 'Sonic the Hedgehog' all hours of the afternoon, drinking capri suns, and laughing at each other until we'd fall out of our chairs! He'd eventually introduce me to all of the neighborhood kids. I met so many kids down at the playground that were of all ethnicities. One kid, Quintin, made it clear that he was the "leader" of Spring Valley, thus owning two chapters of the "Power Rangers Social Club." He was always the Black Ranger!

I fit in perfectly with them there. About twenty of us boys would gather together around three thirty each afternoon, to practice for imaginary battles, until the girls pulled us away to play "Hide and Go Seek" or until someone got hurt; whichever came first.

It was perfect.

We got dirty, we ran and laughed, and chased the local girls around from park to park; we helped neighbors carry groceries, threw rocks at imaginary intruders to the neighborhood, and shared walkie talkie conversations from either side of the development. The only enemies that we had besides the imaginary creatures coming to invade our complex, were our parents, who often came to find us when it got too dark to play anymore.

Alvin and Quintin came to get me everyday. And when it rained, we went to each other's houses and played indoors. Alvin's house was usually always calm, unless his sister Rosa was home. Rosa was sixteen and beautiful! She was short and slim with long dark hair, and looked like a younger version of Ms. Maritza. She went to Spring Valley High School, and dated an older kid that drove a sports car. But Rosa didn't listen. She'd always use her mother's inability to communicate in english against her. Rosa could get away with so much just by speaking in English very fast so her mother didn't have time to mentally translate, or very low so that she didn't have time to hear. Sometimes, she would leave the house and be gone for days with no one knowing where she was. Ms. Maritza would even have to get the police department involved in finding her. I knew when Alvin was worried about his sister, because his stutter became more apparent. One night, when it stormed so bad that the lights went out in our entire building, Alvin sat in my living room, and explained to my mother and me, about how he, his mom and sister were once homeless in Texas. His mother used heroin as her drug of choice. He said that Rosa was older while his mother was in the throws of her addiction, and that she'd seen too much. He cried to us several times, trying to reinact the delicate memories. I felt for him, because I understood. Alvin said that one day he woke up in a shelter with the hiccups, and a stutter, that never went away. He and Rosa ended up in foster care too, but separated. He said that ever since they'd

reunited with their mother, Rosa has never been the same.

She held so much anger and resentment towards Ms.

Maritza for her addiction and for allowing them to go into

the system. Although they were together now, Rosa hadn't

forgiven her mother. Whenever Alvin spoke, I listened

attentively, and imagined what it must've been like for him

and Rosa.

One day in August, Alvin, Quintin, and I were

playing a new game on the TV in his living room when we

heard a heavy thud at the front door. We opened the door to

find Rosa lying on the floor with blood pouring from her

nose!!

Alvin screamed, "Mami!!!!"

Quintin and I dragged her into the house and locked

the door. She laid on the floor crying as Ms. Maritza came

to her side talking to her in spanish.

It wasn't until the paramedics came that Quintin and I understood what happened. Alvin cried to us, as they lifted her onto the stretcher, and out of the door. My mother held Ms. Maritza as they put Rosa into the ambulance to take her to the hospital.

They said that she'd been raped by some friends of her boyfriend from the summer school she was attending. Quinton and I didn't know what that word meant until Alvin explained it to us. Alvin stayed at my house for the weekend while Ms. Maritza stayed in town with Rosa at the hospital. It was a very sad time for all of us.

When Rosa came home after being in the hospital for a few days, we had a small party with balloons and cake. She seemed happy to see us all. She thanked me and Mommy for being there for Alvin and Ms. Maritza.

Alvin had become my brother. A brother like Shawn and Mike were. He had my back, and I had his. By the time that school started, Alvin and I had developed a strong bond and we were always together. Naturally, we rode the bus together, with Quintin tagging along somewhere not too far behind. We started fifth grade together, and on a mission; to always be there for each other! My rank in our club had been promoted to Blue Ranger, which was almost Black Ranger. Life was sweet; Saturday morning cartoons, Mommy taking Shay and I bowling on Saturday nights, and I was adjusting great to the new school!

Until one Saturday night, in the fall, when Mommy introduced me to her new "friend," Mr Rodney. He was tall, and wore a high-top fade. Mr. Rodney was also in recovery and they'd met in an NA meeting. I didn't like it. I never wanted anyone in our house. I never wanted another man around Mommy. It was just too risky. Mommy's weakness was men. And because he was in recovery too, if anything happened, it would be so easy for Mommy to relapse and everything would change for all of us. Even though Mr. Rodney never moved in with us, he was there when I would try to get in Mommy's bed on Saturday mornings to watch cartoons, or on Friday nights when we were supposed to talk about how the week was for us.

But I still had Alvin, and now, Rosa, who was doing so much better now; she'd even stopped running away. She went to school each day, and her attitude towards her brother and mother was improving. Anytime Mr. Rodney was there, after I knew that Shay was asleep, I would go over to Alvin's, who always left the front door open for me. Always.

"Hola, Devin!!" said Rosa, who was sitting in the living room cuddling with her new strange pet ferret. She named him Sosa, and he ran all through the house. Alvin and I played with him until 9:30 that night; when Ms. Maritza asked if I was staying over or going home. I told her that I was going home, and told Alvin I would see him in the morning for school.

Quintin knocked on my door while I was brushing my teeth that Thursday morning.

"We gon' miss the bus if you don't hurry boy!!" shouted an impatient Quintin.

"Bye, Momma." I whispered into her dark bedroom just before leaving, and locking the front door. Quintin was already knocking on Alvin's door, but to no avail.

"He must be sleeping good!" laughed Quintin, before tightening his straps to his backpack.

"Come on, let's just go, he's prolly gon' meet us there." I said to Quintin. We ran to the bus stop and stepped onto the cold bus just before it pulled away.

Our cold knuckles banged on his door that afternoon until the door rattled. Neither of us had seen Alvin in school that day at all, and now we were worried. Nobody had seen him, and he wasn't at the club meeting that evening either. It felt weird. Something was up. My mother called Ms. Maritza, and knocked on her door too. Nothing.

It was strange. The next evening, Friday evening, Quintin and I banged on Alvin's door until a maintenance man walked up to us in the hallway.

"Sorry boys, gotta get past you," he said.

"Wait, where are they??" I asked.

"They not home!" said Quintin quickly.

"Oh, nah boys, they done moved out," said the maintenance man.

"MOVED OUT??" we said in chorus.

"Yup. They gone, fellas," he said and disappeared after jingling several different keys into the keyhole.

I sat at dinner that evening, quiet, clawing at my scalloped potatoes while Shay screamed out, "one, two, thu-three," mocking the owl on the Tootsie Roll commercial that had just went off.

"It's just so strange 'cus she ain't even say nothin' to me either," said Mommy.

That was the last time that I'd ever see my friend again. Like Shawn and Mike, he was gone forever. Lost in my memory to the point that I questioned if they'd ever even lived there at all. Within the month, a white family moved into their old apartment. Strange.

Chapter 24

I started going over to Quintin's house almost every night through the winter. The bitter cold evenings made us stay indoors enough for me to get to know his family. Quintin had a younger sister we all called "Pat," which was short for "Patricia," her given name. She was named after her mother and was about six years old, with dark skin, and either thick poof balls or ponytails, and she looked just like their older brother Anthony. Ms. Patricia was the exact same age as my mother, and struggled with drugs like Mommy did. She was short, and usually very fun to be around. But you could tell she'd been through some things. "Her moods can change like the wind!" Quintin would always say. Sometimes, when Ms. Patricia was talking, you'd see her go off somewhere else in her mind. She would have a far away look as if she was someplace else.

There were many times when she was happy and laughing and having a good time, but then, out of nowhere, she'd put everybody out of her house. "Change like the wind."

Anthony was Quintin's older brother. He was 14, and never let us forget it. He was dark skinned, like Ms. Patricia, very athletic and loved to play football. Anthony was usually pretty cool when he wasn't ball busting us younger kids. He looked out for us all. Their father was Mr. Jerome, and he was always nice to us. He loved his family, and worked hard. He worked construction, and often did odd jobs around the neighborhood. They were the only two parent household out of all of my friends in the complex.

Once Alvin left, Quintin and I started hanging out a lot more. Our mothers had been pretty close already, so it just made sense for us to hang out more. Ms. Patricia started coming up to our place on Saturday nights, to hang out with my mother and Ms. Kelly.

I don't know where Ms. Kelly came from or how my mother knew her, but one day she was just showed up with Mommy. She was a pretty woman but she liked to party. She came over on the weekends and always had a different man with her. Ms. Kelly was full of drama and always knew the latest gossip. They would play cards, smoke cigarettes and drink wine coolers or beer and listen to music. Ms. Kelly always bought the beer. I always felt uneasy when I saw her. She was a very provocative woman always dancing and grinding around the house. She didn't have any kids and it showed in her reckless behavior; always drunk and arguing with whatever man she had with her. She was a classless hoochie and was a bad influence on Mommy. She always had make-up caked on her face, and liquor on her breath. I did not like her one bit.

I would always see the trio setting up for their weekly ritual as I was leaving out to sleepover at Quintin's that spring. Mr Jerome would always ask, "Hey, Devin, who all up at y'all house?"

"Same as always." I'd reply.

As time went on, it seemed that Ms. Patricia liked being at my house more than her own.

Quintin and I walked all the way into town on a misty Saturday morning to go to Blockbuster Video. We'd heard all about this cartoon movie in school called, "The Lion King" and couldn't wait to see it. We both pretended that we didn't want to see it, well, because it was a cartoon movie, and that stuff was for little kids, not big boys like us.

"We gon' have to watch it at your house!" screamed Q from the other side of the road.

"My momma ain't gon' wanna do that! It's Saturday, they night, remember?" I shouted back.

We threw rocks at each other in the pouring rain from both sides of Two Notch Road. It took us an hour to get back home, and we were SOAKED. We stopped at the laundromat near the leasing office to get cold sodas from the soda machine for twenty- five cents.

"Momma, it's just so we can watch the new videos that we picked up, and we the only ones with a VCR!!" I whined.

Mommy looked up from the pepper steak she was making, and said, "Well, that's fine, I don't need no company this weekend anyway. You better let Shay watch, too."

Q and I ran to my room in danced and cheered while I changed into dry clothes. After changing, we went to his house, packed his sleeping bag and were heading out to my house, when Ms. Patricia told me to tell Mommy that she'd be over around seven.

"Oh, Ms. Pat, she said she not havin' no company over tonight. See, we gon' have our sleepover at my house." I said.

"Mama, they got a VCR over there!" Quintin interrupted.

She looked sad for a moment, like what we said changed her whole mood. Anthony threw dry spaghetti noodles at us from the kitchen while he talked on the broken house phone. She waved us out, and we flew out the door.

We sat in the living room all day, watching a Power Rangers marathon, and even saw a couple of episodes of "C-Bear and Jamal", an urban cartoon featuring Tone Loc. Mommy and Shay walked up to Piggly Wiggly with us to get snacks.

"What's a good movie without.." Mommy asked.

"Pop-corn!!" we all screamed in unison.

"Pop Khans!" shouted Shay from inside her rain poncho.

We laughed and sang "100 Bottles of Beer on the Wall" to the store and back.

The movie was awesome. It was funny, and we even sang along with some of the songs. I cried a little when Mufasa died. I played it off by acting like I had to pee in the bathroom. I think Quintin did too. When it finally went off, he laughed at me, saying he saw me tear up. Shay was asleep, and Mommy was at the door telling Ms. Kelly that tonight was guy's night. We fell asleep eating popcorn and Steak-ums, while watching "Cops" reruns.

I woke up to the phone ringing and it rang three times before I actually got up to answer it. I knew that it was early because nobody else was awake to hear the phone ringing.

"He-Hello." I asked in a raspy voice.

"Yeah, Devin, where D at?" asked a panicking Mr. Jerome.

"She sleep, Mr. Jerome." I answered.

"Go get her up and tell Quintin to come home, NOW!!" he screamed.

"Ok-Ok, yes, sir," I said. By the time I put the phone down, Quintin sat up straight in his sleeping bag with a puzzled look.

"Yo Daddy said get home right now. I don't know what happened, but get home!" I shouted.

Quintin looked frustrated, but immediately began collecting himself. I ran into Mommy's room, knocking on the door, just in case she had "company" over. But she didn't so I ran in to tell her what was going on.

"Momma, Mr. Jer-Jerome, say he need you to get the phone. Sound like something wrong!!"

Mommy started moving towards the kitchen without even asking anything. I could tell that she was surprised and not even awake yet.

"Yeah, Rome, What's…what?" There was a long pause while she listened to him explain what happened. "Oh damn, shit, Ok, Rome!" She slammed down the phone when Q ran out of the door. She looked like something was very wrong.

"Look in on Shay, Devin, I be back." she said, grabbing her robe off the corner of her bed post.

"But Ma, wh- what happened?" I asked running behind her to the door.

"Just keep an eye on Shay!" she said, running down the steps into the crisp air.

I looked out the patio window to watch Mommy run to their building, and then she was gone. I looked into Shay's room, where she was sleeping hard. The night's festivities must've really worn her out. I waited by the patio window, hoping to see a sign of either Quintin or Mommy, but fifteen minutes had gone by and I was biting my nails. I grabbed the spare key out of the second drawer in the kitchen, and locked the front door behind me. I needed to know what was going on.

I got to their door and could hear whimpering from the living room. I knocked very soft on the door, and nobody even came to it. I turned the doorknob slowly and entered into the apartment. Anthony sat on the couch, rocking back and forth, like in a daze.

"What's goin' on, Ant? You alright?" I asked quietly.

He didn't even look at me. He was like in a trance or something with his fists balled up over a football he had resting in his lap. I heard voices from the master bedroom in the back; multiple voices. I walked down the hallway, past the kids' rooms, straight to Ms. Pat and Mr. Rome's room. I saw Mommy and Mr. Rome struggling to pick Ms. Pat up off the floor. I gasped at her condition. She was mumbling some type of gibberish, while Mommy was pulling her clothes back onto her.

"Devin, get them kids outta here for me, man. Please!" thundered Mr. Jerome. He had tears in his eyes, and looked very discombobulated.

"Yes, sir," I whispered.

Mommy looked over her shoulder at me, and motioned for me to get the kids together. I walked back to Q's room where he sat holding Pat, crying. I walked over to the two of them and just hugged them for a moment. Quintin's body went limp in my arms when I held the two of them. He sobbed, almost uncontrollably, for a long time.

"Come on y'all, lets go on up to my house." I said.

I grabbed Pat's hand while Quintin wiped off his face. We walked into the living room where Jerome was kneeling down, eye level in front of Anthony, who was now physically shaking and crying himself. Quintin and I escorted him out the door and into the cold. It wasn't until we all were back in my house and with Pat tucked into Shay's room, that they even started to speak.

"Momma was in there drinkin' mouthwash again," said Q.

"MOUTH-WASH??" I questioned.

"Yeah, she been used to do that a long time ago. When it ain't no liquor, she drinks mouthwashes," he said.

I shook my head like I understood, but I was still extremely confused. Mouthwash? What the heck could mouthwash do to get you drunk, I wondered.

Apparently, drinking mouthwash can make you very sick, and can put you down for a few days while you throw up the lining of your stomach. That's what I heard Mommy say to somebody on the phone later that night. Ms. Patricia was so upset that Mommy wasn't having company over, that she decided to have a party on her own. A party that left her kids and husband razzled. Her bipolar tendencies had come back and it was a sad couple of weeks for my friends. It was hard to watch. But Mommy was there for her.

Mommy would let Anthony, Q, and Pat come to our house after school for dinner every night for almost three weeks, which made me happy because Quintin was always over. And Mommy played a good hero. I was so proud of her.

Chapter 25

Mommy and Mr. Jerome were walking very slowly with Ms. Patricia in front of them. We slowed down just in front of my building to get a drink of water from the hose attached to the wall. It was starting to get hot out, and we were tired. Quintin, Adam, and Jessie, two white boys from the neighborhood, followed me over to the hose, panting heavily from exhaustion. The three adults emerged on the curb when I realized that Ms. Patricia had a bandana over her eyes, and a huge smile on her face.

"Alright now Pat, no peekin' girl!" shouted Mommy with a huge grin on her own face.

"Baby, now I want you to watch yo step," said Mr. Jerome. Quintin tapped me, and looked happily over at his parents.

"One, two, three!!" shouted Mommy and Mr. Jerome.

Ms. Patricia opened her eyes, and blinked them very fast to adjust to the light. And looked confused. Almost dazed. Mr. Jerome held out his hand to her with two sparkling silver keys.

"Baby, I know it ain't no new car, but it's your car!" said Mr. Jerome.

Ms. Patricia started crying instantly. Mommy rubbed her shoulders from behind as she and Mr. Jerome hugged next to the big green car. It was truly an awesome moment to witness. After the ordeal they just went through, it was nice to see them smile.

All of us stood on the curb as she started it up for the first time. Her smile beamed clear through the windshield! Within a week, Ms. Patricia asked Mommy to come on down to the hotel where she'd worked, and come work some late shifts with her. She always told Mommy that she wanted to be able to pay her back for being there for her little family. Mr. Rodney hated the idea of Mommy being gone overnight because he knew the friends Mommy was hanging out with. He knew that Ms. Kelly always had men around and if they came with drugs, he knew Mommy could easily relapse. But I loved it! No more Ms. Kelly coming over drunk, and unannounced, no more Mr. Rodney staying over and calling all day, either!

It was perfect!

When Mommy got her first paycheck, she treated us all to Shoney's one Saturday night. Me, Shay, Quintin, Ms. Patricia, Mr. Jerome, Pat, and Anthony all piled into the big green Buick, and ate all that we could at the buffet. We ate bacon, shrimp, pasta, ribs, pizza, steak, and chicken. I was asleep before we made it back to the development. Mommy asked me to take Shay in the house and said that she and Ms. Patricia were heading down to play cards with some of their work friends.

"You sure, Momma? It's Saturday night." I asked reluctantly. They usually gathered at my house on Saturday nights. It was easier for me to keep an eye on her that way. I didn't feel helpless when I could see what was going on.

Mommy shooed me into the house with a wavering hand. I felt uneasy watching the Buick pull off so fast, as I carried Shay into the apartment. I stood by the patio window and thought about what Mommy could be doing, not falling asleep until two in the morning when she finally came home.

***

Walking home from the bus stop that Monday, I told Quinton all about how I waited up all night until Mommy came home. He seemed just as confused as I was as to why they were out so late.

"Two o'clock?" shouted Quintin as he walked in the direction of his building.

"Two o'clock!" I shouted back to him as I fought with the front door key to open the knob. "That's what time they come in!"

I opened the front door, to find a smiling Mr. Rodney and Mommy at the dining room table with a huge yellow bag sitting in front of them.

"Hey, Wha-what's that?" I asked.

Mommy got up and gave me a hug. "How was your day, baby?" she asked with a sly smirk on her face.

"It was good, Momma!" I shouted, and pointed to the bag on the table. "What's that?!" I shrieked.

"It's yours, baby." I cautiously walked over and opened the bag. I couldn't believe what was inside!

"A SUPER NINTENDO!!" I screamed.

I ran over and hugged Mommy with a tight clench, and thanked her.

"You better thank Rodney. He the one wanted you to have it." Mommy said.

"Thank you, Mr. Rod.."

"Ain't no need, you been doin' good." he interrupted. I hugged him too, and ran back to the bag. I unpacked the system, and with about 10 minutes of careful connections, hooked it up to the TV, that I moved carefully to the dining room table, "The Super Mario Brothers" theme song blared from the blown speaker of the television.

My eyes filled with tears once Mommy and Mr. Rodney left the room, and I held my controller in my hand. It was mine. My very own game system! I hadn't had a game system since the Atari that Mommy "borrowed" back in the Party House in Baltimore. I felt Complete. Content.

I felt important.

Quintin came over to play the game with me everyday after school for a week straight. We only had one controller and one game, but we didn't mind sharing. Mr. Rodney was always there when we came home. Mommy would always come in with Ms. Pat waiting just outside to

take Quintin home in their car.

Chapter 26

"Come on, Dee!!" Ms. Pat said. "We just gon' go play some spades and talk some trash at Trish Ann's house." she continued.

"Girrrll, I don't feel like leaving back out, it's too damn hot outside!!" Mommy shouted back from the bathroom, washing her hands and face in the sink.

"Just for a lil' while!" Ms. Pat shouted back, picking lint balls from Quintin's choppy fade.

"Come on, man, it's gon' be fun. They got a big yard for exploring in the woods." Quintin whispered.

I fell into a hole on the game, and turned it off in frustration.

"OKAYYYY!!" Mommy shrieked.

I walked out with Shay and told Mommy we'd be waiting at Ms. Pat's.

Shay picked at her dolls hair in the back seat of the Buick, while Anthony tried to teach Quintin and I yet another one of his magic tricks that he'd been practicing.

"Pick a card, any card!!" He hummed.

Quintin looked at me and laughed, crossing his eyes, while Anthony guessed the wrong card for the third time.

We jerked hard as Ms. Pat pulled into the liquor store parking lot for beers and cigarettes.

"It gotta be the two of hearts, now." Anthony groaned. Q, Shay and I burst into laughter at how hard Anthony was trying to concentrate. It was hilarious to see his sweaty face and bulging eyes search through the entire deck countless times always to get it wrong.

Chapter 27

We pulled up to what appeared to be a large sized shack, at the end of the block, two rights off of Two Notch Road. The Buick didn't have air conditioning and we were all hot, sweaty, and ready to get out.

"Hey, y'all!" yelled Ms. Trish-Ann from the rickety doorway of the house. She was a middle-aged, slim, white woman with stringy brown hair and dirty bare feet. She spoke with a cigarette dangling from her dry lips as we walked up.

"Hey, Trish, where the rest of the girls at?" beamed Ms. Pat, who seemed unphased by the sweltering May heat.

We walked inside the old house, and saw a table with three other women sitting there with a boombox blasting nearby. There was a thick haze and a familiar aroma. The smell was straight from the Party House, lots of cigarette smoke and weed in the air. Mommy kneeled down handing me a bag full of Huggies juices and chips.

"Y'all go and have some fun with the other kids, baby." she whispered.

I looked her in her eyes as she walked over to the table quickly. I was looking for that connection that we had. I was looking for silent confirmation that she was gonna be alright in there. I was looking for safety. I saw Ms. Kelly wave, and mouth something to me, but I couldn't hear over the loud music playing.

By the time I got out the door, Quintin and Anthony had already opened a bag of the chips, and were throwing rocks off of the edge of the driveway. Shay sat on the edge of the porch with her dolls, having a conversation amongst them. She smiled when I opened her juice, and a little white girl, who looked to be about five, came in between us, with a naked Barbie doll to play with Shay. Ms. Trish-

Ann hollered from the house that the little girl was her daughter and needed someone to play with.

I walked away from them, and ran over to the driveway with the other boys. Quintin, Anthony and I were accompanied by Shane, Ms. Trish-Ann's son. We decided to try and play a game of catch with a football from one side of the house, to the other.

"Go LONG!!" shouted an energized Shane. He, too, was barefoot, and came up with the idea to throw the football over the whole house. Quintin and I were on teams, and stood at the front of the house, where the little kids were still playing.

"Well, where did it go!" Anthony shouted.

Shane had thrown the ball over the house, and into the woods that sat next to Ms. Trish -Ann's property, and now it was lost. We all poked in between the branches and bushes that made the border into the woods.

"DAMN!" screamed Quintin.

We ran over to where he was, only to see trickles of blood coming from his forearm, clear indication of the "Rose Bush" Shane said as we walked up. Anthony carefully picked the prickly pieces from his brother's arm, when Shane pointed to the roof of their house.

"Well, let's go!" he said, shaking his head.

"Go where?' I asked, frantically swiping at the swarm of gnats from around my head.

"To the MOOON!" sang Shane, marching like a soldier towards the house.

Anthony made a swirling motion with his finger next to his own head, to say "this kid is crazy." His bulging eyes, again, made Quintin and I laugh hysterically as we followed. I noticed that the girls were still laughing and playing safely on the front porch, and I flashed Shay a "thumbs up." She smiled, and went back to playing with Becca.

"Gotta hold on tight." grunted Shane, who's slowly climbing up the back pillar of the house with dirty hands, and sweat dripping from his forehead.

"I ain't goin' up there!" proclaimed Quintin as he watched Shane slowly inch up towards the middle of the pillar.

"Well, I am!" said Anthony proudly.

He grabbed high on the pillar, and pulled his body halfway up in one powerful motion, just as Shane got his entire body up onto the flat roof.

"SEE!! I TOLD Y'ALL!! THE MOON!!" shouted Shane from the top.

I looked back at Quintin, who was now standing at full attention waiting for me to start climbing.

"Here goes nothing." I laughed, as I reached out for the pillar and began climbing. I grunted as I pulled my legs to my chest, and realized that this wasn't as easy as Anthony and Shane made it look. I grabbed onto what felt like large nails on the backside of the pillar that were completely out of sight. I realized that if I swung my body around, I could use them as tiny steps to help me brace for my next big push. As I swung my body around, I realized the nails were just wide enough for my feet to rest on and that my face was just above the bathroom window of the house. I looked down at a nervous Quintin, and decided to take a breath. Out of the corner of my eye, I saw a small flash inside the house. I squinted to see past the dirt on the outside of the window, and saw another small flash, like a, a flicker. Shane and Anthony called out to me as I paused just long enough to look inside the window.

The women stood, in plain sight. Ms. Pat was shielding the flame for Mommy to light a clear, small pipe. A thick, white smoke emerged from Mommy's lips, before I saw Ms. Pat hit the pipe for herself. What I saw temporarily dazed me. It stunned me enough to forget my grasp on the pillar, and I slipped clean off. I hit the ground softly, and didn't even try to break my fall.

"You, alright bruh?" Quintin asked, shortly followed by Anthony's voice.

"What happened, is ya hurt?"

"Yeah, I fell." I gasped, looking at both of them in a confused state.

The boys stood me up, relaying the message to Shane that I was ok. Without words, I grabbed Q by the arm and dragged him to the bottom of the bathroom window. We both crouched down, and I told him to look inside. He faced the window with a slight smile still on his face, that I watched fade away almost instantly. My chest tightened. My blood boiled, and I wanted to cry by the time I looked at him again. Quintin backed up with a wide mouth and tears in his eyes.

"What the hell is wrong wit y'all? Move, I'm goin' back up!" whispered Anthony.

"Look in the window, Ant." I said calmly, not even looking at him. Anthony came over to the window, panting heavily and pushed us out of the way, so he could get a better look. He didn't need to get on his tippy toes because he was already much taller than us. His eyes glossed over, and his smile faded away, too, as he saw the lighter flicking in the distance. He slid away from the window after about a minute. We sat on the ground, dazed and lethargic under the window.

None of us had words to speak, when Shane came down asking, "What's takin' so long? It's hot on the moon when you by ya self!" His stringy hair dripped with sweat.

"FUCK THIS!" I said in a low tone.

I climbed up, wiped the tears from my eyes, and grabbed for the pillar. I climbed up the whole thing this time without the nails in the back. I wiggled up the pillar keeping my eyes away from the window, and panted with RAGE, and anger. Within seconds, I was all the way up on the roof. I took deep breaths as I scoured the edge, to see Quintin reaching for my hand.

"I'm gon' do it!!" I said looking into his eyes.

"What we doing?" he said, wiping his pants off.

"I'm gon' kill myself." I whispered, looking out over the front of the roof.

"Me, too, then! Fuck it, they don't care non' ' bout us!!" screamed Quintin.

He stared at me with tears bubbling in his eyes, and sweat popping from his forehead. I cupped my hands and wiped my face, clearing my nose. I took a deep breath, and stared at the cloudy blue sky. Quintin banged his chest, and mumbled something too low for me to hear. Anthony's fingertips touched the roof, as I backed up to the edge. Quintin looked over at me, and walked towards me with his chest out. Anthony spoke something to us, but I couldn't hear him. I didn't want to hear him. We crouched down into a racer's position and counted.

"One."

I closed my eyes, and cleared my mind.

"Two."

I saw Shay and Ms. Ruby.

"Three"

I saw my grandmother and my mother at a time before I was even born, smiling at each other through the rear-view mirror of my grandmother's Volkswagen bus.

We pushed off on our toes at the same time. I gasped the deepest breath I'd ever taken by the third thrust. Quintin reached out ahead of me and Anthony on the fifth thrust. I felt like a bird by the sixth. We were in the air by the seventh.

Anthony's scream echoed deep into my ears as I felt the wind rush past my face. It was over. Quintin squealed in the air. I lost control of my limbs. The wind flapped my cheeks, and soothed my soul. Rapid slowness. My spirit was free.

***

Other than the school bus, or in the hallways, it had been two weeks since I'd been allowed to hang out with Q. Our mothers decided that we might need some time away from each other, at least for a little while. Despite the reasons behind our suicide attempt, my mother didn't want me to be around him. She knew why we jumped off of that roof; both of them knew. But neither one of them wanted to take responsibility for the part they played. It wasn't important enough to them. So, they blamed us, the kids.

Two weeks, and a lot of silence later, I watched her parade around the house on a Monday night in a full sweat. She had company over, and they were playing cards and talking. I went to the kitchen to get a cup of water, and was greeted by the familiar, thick haze of crack smoke, cigarettes and weed. The adults scrambled to hide their paraphernalia as they heard me padding down the hall.

"Hhe-y Dev, uh-uhgh, you want some-some-something to drink?" she gasped in a jumpy, but raspy voice.

I didn't even respond. I looked at her glistening face as her jaw jerked all around. She was always like that when she was high. Her words twisted out of her mangled mouth, and her eyes looked as if they were gonna pop out of her head at any moment. They called that "geeked out". I shook my head walking out of the kitchen at the pitiful scene, not even getting the water that I came for.

I walked to my room and opened the screen to my window as wide as it would go. I hated the smell. The smell always made me gag with anger, rage, and disgust. Ever since the Party House, I hated that smell. I stared out into the pine trees that lined the back of our development and wondered if they saw the same things as me. Maybe if I stood still there long enough, I could turn into one of them. And I'd be replaced by one of them. My thoughts ran through my mind like big city traffic; fast and chaotic.

The next day after school, Quintin asked me to help him off the bus. The soft cast was ready to be removed from his ankle. I sneered at the dirty plaster as it neared my face when he climbed down. The cast was a reminder of the Friday night when everything changed for us. He and I walked home in silence. I chewed on a popsicle stick from last period at school, when Q asked me:

"Think Ms. Dee gon' let me come back over this weekend?" I heard the tremble in his voice and understood why immediately.

See, Mr. Jerome knew that Ms. Pat had been at my house almost every night. And he needed to be able to keep tabs on his wife's actions when she was out of sight. She had apparently made a habit of doing "whatever" when it came to drugs. He needed Q to be able to come back over.

I shook my head at the thought and just said, "Yeah."

We shook hands and separated when I climbed the steps to my building. I went inside our apartment, and it was silent. I looked around, heard no television, or saw Shay walking around. The house looked clean, and the patio blinds let in the late spring sunshine. I ran through to my room, dropped my bookbag, and decided that I wanted to play Super Mario until somebody came home. The mood just seemed right. I walked to the kitchen to make a peanut butter and jelly sandwich, all the while humming the tune of Tevin Campbell's "Can We Talk". I was in a great mood! I sat down to the dining room table, turned on the small television set sitting atop, went to reach for-- and then it hit me. My game system was gone! My heart dropped, and I felt my chest get tight as I walked around the dining room looking for the box that it had come in. I knew immediately that it had been sold. I threw the other half of my sandwich away as my thoughts interrupted my appetite. I walked into my room, stretched out across my bed, and cried myself into a deep, dark pit. I couldn't believe she would do me like that. Like she didn't care about how it would make me feel.

She had quit her job, she was back to drinking, smoking crack, and bringing strange men into our home again, almost every single night. It was so embarrassing. When Friday came, Quintin and I stood in the living room holding our sleeping bags. I tried not to tear up in embarrassment when we turned on the lights to see that both our living room sofa, and love seat were gone. You could see the outlines of the furniture still in the carpet, indicating its recent departure. Even though she knew that I was having company over, she didn't cancel her get together. She and Ms. Pat were in her bedroom with the door closed, along with three men that I'd never seen before. Although, the five of them spoke loudly, I couldn't make out what was being said. All I heard was a bunch of drug induced, inaudible sounds.

Quintin and I tipped to my room quietly, and grabbed the blankets off my bed for our living room "fort."

"What you wan' be when you grow up, Devin?" whispered Quintin.

I looked in his direction and said the only thing that came to mind.

"Alive."

He thought for a moment, and reached out his hand for me to shake.

"Me too." he said, just before rolling over into his sleeping bag and drifting to sleep.

Chapter 28

The following day was a bright Saturday morning. Quintin was gone by the time I had woke up, and Shay was wrapped in the blankets that was our "fort" from the night before. I slapped her knee as I got up off of the carpet and turned the TV on for her.

"I wanna eat!" she shouted.

"Give me a sec, Shay, I gotta pee!" I said jogging down the hallway to the bathroom. I peered into the cracked door of mommy's room, and counted five sleeping bodies; three on the floor under one blanket, and two in the rickety bed. The room stank of sweat, smoke and liquor. Mommy was on her bed with a dark-skinned man who was completely naked. Ms. Pat was rolled into a heap on the floor with a man at each side. The sight made my stomach turn. I remember when it was just Mommy and Mr.

Rodney in that room, but he left her when she started using again. I guess he didn't want to risk his own sobriety.

After leaving the bathroom, I went into the kitchen and made Shay a baggie of dry cereal because there wasn't any milk for me to make her a bowl. Coming back into the living room, I noticed a small box that read, "Strong Fragrance Incense Cones," across the front. Curiosity made me read the box, and open it, to find eight small burgundy cones. The directions said to "light and keep away from all things flammable." I'd seen Mommy use these before, and this was a perfect way to get the smell out of our apartment. I went back into the kitchen, and dug into the junk drawer where there were all types of paraphernalia held; lighters, matches, aluminium foil, steel wool, and broken Bic pens. I grabbed a lighter and flicked it near the tip. The cone sparked quickly and I blew out the glowing ember like I'd seen Mommy do before. The smoke smelled of an overpowering musk, but I felt better nonetheless. I sat next to Shay on the floor, and decided to open the patio blinds, to let in some natural sunshine. When I backed away from the blinds, I started dancing to The Power Rangers theme song on the TV. I felt something hot hit my elbow and immediately fanned it off. It was the incense! It had fallen down from the top of the TV, burned my elbow and had burned a hole STRAIGHT THROUGH THE CARPET!! I shrieked in fear, and felt more scared than I had in a LONG time.

"Ooohhhhhhhhh" hummed Shay.

"Shut up." I mouthed to her, with tears in my eyes. No matter how much water I put on the hole, the carpet was melted in the shape of the cone. Panicking, I hurried and rushed clothes on Shay and me, and ran to Quintin's house. I told Quintin that I needed to leave Shay there for a while, because I knew that Mommy would kill me for what I did to her floor. Q said that he would come with me, but I left while he went to brush his teeth. I was too scared to sit still. I ran across the development. I ran past Spring Valley High School. I jogged past the pizzeria, and walked by Winn Dixie. By the time I made it to Two Notch Road, I was exhausted, but grateful to have so much space between my mother and me. I walked until I came up on the Walmart, a half mile later.

"Never been so happy to see a soda machine." I mumbled to myself, walking across the parking lot.

The lot was busy with well- to- do white folks, all seeming to look right past me. I waited in line behind an old man just in front of the "25 cents" sign. There was a table of Girl Scouts selling cookies next to the entrance. I couldn't hear what they were saying, but they all looked so clean, and happy. Their blue eyes gleamed with every person that walked by.

I slowly sipped my Sam's Club cola while I walked down each aisle. By the time I made it to the electronics section, I had completely forgotten all about what happened back at home. I was happy, my core temperature had returned to normal, and I was in one of my favorite places in the world.

The sign boasted "NEW AND IN COLOR!" in bright red letters. It had Mario jumping through the letters with bright colors that spelled out GAMEBOY. I was astonished, simply astonished at how dope it all was. The associate laughed at me as I stood in the middle of the aisle.

"Hey, man, I'm guessing you'd like to play the Loud Collection." he said with a smile.

I shook my head with my mouth gaped open. The boxes themselves were made of clear plastic, so you could see the different colors of the system. Now, I had always wanted a Gameboy, but this was just outrageous! The colors were so bold, and popped right through the packaging.

"Here man, look at all of them." He handed me the boxes that he had stacked next to the glass cases he was loading them into.

They were made in red, green, black, yellow, white, blue, and clear. He shouted from behind the counter, "We shoulda been had 'em, but they said the release kept gettin pushed back, so we're just gettin 'em almost two months later!"

The transparent one was my favorite. I thought it just genius that it was designed to show you the inner workings! I loved to see how it worked! I sat down on the floor reading the box, with my soda in my lap. The overhead speaker called for an Electronics phone call, so the worker walked away.

'*That guy is gone, and you can just take it*!' I thought to myself, but I knew it wasn't right. Even though I wanted it really, really bad, it still wasn't the right thing to do. I walked around staring at the many cameras in the ceiling, and felt like crying. Why couldn't I just take it? I knew other kids that did stuff like that all the time? I deserved it after all that I had to deal with, so why couldn't I just do it? 'Because you know better.' I heard Mimi's voice ring through my ears as clearly as if she were standing in front of me. I put my hand on the Mario poster on the sliding glass door as I walked out of the front door, leaving the Gameboy where it was. I felt sad again. I watched two white girls take pictures near the Girl Scout table. They were cheerleaders setting up for a fundraiser. The sun seemed to hit them differently. Everybody was smiling or laughing, soft air blowing through their hair. The parents came out with different color freeze pops for everybody as they unloaded from the yellow school bus. I stood next to the soda machines and looked down at my shoes. I decided that even though I had just enough change for one more soda to take home, I didn't want to. I walked home, drifting in and out of reality. I imagined that I was one of those white kids getting back on that bus, playing with my new,

clear, Gameboy, with white skin, blonde hair, blue eyes,

cool sunglasses, with my hat turned backwards and NO

cares in the world! I could feel the plastic in my hands,

while my "Mom" played in my hair calling me Kiddo. My

name would be Connor. Yeah, Connor. Connor would wear

new high tops everyday, he was popular, and the epitome

of cool. He played almost every sport so he had friends

everywhere. And his house was dope! He had two

Gameboys, and posters of Michael Jackson on the walls of

his bedroom. Lots of windows and high ceilings! I would

have the latest boombox in my room, and a fish tank. My

parents would feed us fresh fruits and vegetables from the

garden in the backyard, and we'd talk about our day during

dinner. Dad was a banker, and Mom was a therapist. They

always made time for me and Megan, my little sister. They

read to us every night, and tucked us in before bed. My

Grandpa and Grandma were still together and my entire family hung out together on weekends.

Connor wasn't here though. He wasn't trying to cross the busy street back to the apartments of Spring Valley, with the sun blazing on his skin. I was. My fantasy was merely a mirage. I had been gone for three hours, and it was time for me to face the music. I walked to my house and opened the door. My stomach wasn't in knots, and I wasn't even nervous anymore. I was numb. I walked around the entire apartment, to see that nobody was there. I walked to Mommy's room, and she wasn't there. Nobody was. I locked the house back up, and walked down to Q's house. I heard everybody before I even got all the way up to the door. I didn't bother knocking, I walked right in, and saw everybody gathered in the living room listening to the radio.

"We gon' have a barbeque." Quintin whispered to me under the loud music. I saw Shay dancing in between Mommy's legs while she talked to Ms. Pat in the kitchen.

"Your grandmother 'bout to call back for you in a half hour!" Mommy shouted from the kitchen. Now it made sense as to why she was down here at Ms. Pat's so early. Mimi called! "This is How we Do It", by Montel Jordan, blasted from the speakers outside as I helped Q and Anthony set up the new grill.

About a half hour later, Little Patricia handed me the house phone, saying it was my grandmother. I ran to the bathroom with the cord running behind me and closed the door.

"Hey Mimi!!" I shouted.

"Devin!!" she shrieked.

I was so happy to hear her voice! She said that she had my aunts at the house, and that they were missing us terribly back in Baltimore. After opening greetings and small talk, she cut right to the chase.

"So, honey, how are you and your sister? I see that the phone is off."

"Well, Mimi, it could be better." I said taking a deep breath. I caught my self getting choked up with tears. This was the first time somebody had asked me that in the last six months. I was hesitant to tell her everything because I absolutely was not going back to foster care again.

"Honey, it's ok, please just tell me what's going on over there." she said. Mimi had a way of making you feel safe and comfortable. She made you feel that you could trust her with your innermost secrets and as much as I didn't want to tell her, I believed that she wouldn't put Shay or me in jeopardy of being in the system again.

I could hear her crying. I took another deep breath.

"She getting high again, and it's getting back to how it was before. She not working no more, sleep all day, and don't be worried bout us like that Mimi."

"Ok, baby, well, that's enough said. Don't you worry about a thing, ok?" she said after taking a deep breath of her own.

"Yes ma'am" I said quietly.

I heard her relaying messages to my aunts before handing the phone back off to Mommy. I don't know what was said on the phone between the two of them, but Mommy was on the phone with Mimi for a long time after that.

Chapter 29

Q and I talked about Sunday's Bar-B-Q all week. It was the last week of school, so we barely had to bring books to class. I tried to follow up on any extra assignments that I could though, while everybody else was able to get an early start on summer. My guidance counselor told me that I was failing three of the five classes I had. By Friday, I realized that it was impossible for me to do all of the assignments I had missed during the whole year in one week. So, I stopped trying. I told Q that we would just enjoy our last day being fifth graders and have a great weekend!

"Oohh yeah! Maybe Momma will let us have another barbeque." whispered Q with a grin.

"I don't know, probably when stamps come out!"

"Who knows? Who cares!! We outta school boy!!"

Quintin danced away laughing, and I followed behind him

to his place.

***

I lay on my living room floor on a pallet eating

sunflower seeds with Q, Shay and Little Patricia laughing

that whole Friday night. I loved the company because it

took my mind off the fact that I was gonna fail the fifth

grade. I couldn't believe that I allowed myself to actually

fail a whole grade. Nobody at the school understood how

difficult it was to do homework while your own mother has

strange people over, doing drugs in your damn kitchen.

They didn't understand our lives at all. And it made me

angry. Angry at the situation but mostly, angry at myself.

"Let's play a game of Twister" said Q, interrupting

me from my thoughts.

"Sounds cool to me." I pulled the game box from

under my bed. Mommy had company over and as I walked

back into the living room, I heard weird noises coming from Mommy's bedroom. Another strange and unidentified man was in there. We played twister in the living room, laughing and falling all over each other for what felt like two hours, until we all fell asleep. The front door opened and closed dozens of times, allowing people known and unknown to walk past the invisible kids on the floor.

The sun was bouncing through the dusty blinds when I heard a soft knock at the door. It was Saturday and nobody around here even MOVED until eleven on a Saturday morning. So, whomever it was, was not normal.

"Who is it?" I said groggily.

"Delivery for this address." said a southern voice. I opened the door and almost fainted. It was Mimi!! Mimi grabbed me and shouted, "Devin!!" She picked me up and held me and I started crying on her shoulder. The fact that I was ten years old went out the window and I hugged my grandmother like I myself was a toddler. I couldn't believe she was here!

"What are you doing here Mimi?!" She put me back down in front of the door, and grasped a half woke Shay from the door way. Shay shouted and screamed "Mimi!!" with a huge grin.

"Honey, we are here to get you guys. It's just time. I want you back home with us, this just isn't working anymore." She took a deep breath and wiped the tears from her eyes, and put her hands on my shoulders.

"I bought your uncles, and your aunt with me, ok? We're gonna pack you guys up, and get you outta here. Enough is enough!" She said.

I backed away from her and smiled, both nervous and excited. Quintin and Little Patricia had already started folding up the blankets when we walked back inside. I introduced Mimi to the both of them.

"I have a peppermint for both of you guys!" she said. Mimi kneeled down and gave both of them a hug, thanking them for all that they had done for us.

Mimi immediately drew the blinds back in the living room, and turned on all of the lights in the apartment. Aunt Monica, Uncle Joe, and my cousin Greg, burst through the front door, and I ran to them, giving them hugs.

"We missed y'all so much!" squeezed Aunt Monica.

"We missed y'all too! I can't believe y'all are here!" I shouted. Uncle Joe hugged me hard, and told me and the rest of the kids to wait outside on the steps.

"Mimi wants y'all to go with her for breakfast, but, first she gon' go in there and get your momma up." he said sternly.

"Yes, sir." I said nervously.

I said a tearful goodbye to Q and Little Patricia. I promised him I would come get him before we left for good to tell him when we were leaving. He tried to hold back his tears, but could not.

"I know I'm crying, Devin, but I'm happy for y'all" he whispered.

"I know it, bruh, I know it." I said quietly.

Both of are heads were down as we clapped hands and hugged for what would be the last time of our lives. Shay was still in Aunt Monica's arms, when Greg rushed the dark-skinned man out the front door of the apartment. Uncle Joe pushed the lighter skinned man out, and hit him in the head with a crack pipe as he descended the stairs. I could hear Mommy falling all over the place from outside the front door, while my cousin Greg was talking to her.

Mimi came out, cleared her throat, "Are we ready to eat, honey?"

"Yes, ma'am!" I boasted.

My Uncle Joe was already carrying my bedroom dresser to the U-Haul truck before Shay and I were strapped in the back seat.

"It's ok to roll the windows down, honey!" Mimi said, putting her sunglasses on.

"It's a new day, and I'm just so happy to have you both with ME!" she gleamed.

"Thanks, Mimi." I said with a smile.

Spring Valley Apartments seemed different as we pulled out. Like the sun was just a shade brighter, like the grass was just a shade greener, and the sky was a deeper shade of blue. The wind brushed over my face as I sat back making funny faces at Shay in her car seat. I caught Mimi's smile from the rear view, while I adjusted my seatbelt and it made me smile instantly. Seal's "Kiss from a Rose" flowed gently through the car, as I looked over the roadway, and the lines that I passed so many times before, thanking God for this miracle that I still couldn't believe

was actually happening. I smiled with tears in my eyes.

Feeling Saved.

Feeling Rescued.

Feeling Important.

Made in the USA
Middletown, DE
07 May 2022